Intermediate Classical Guitar Pieces

Compiled and edited by

Dmitrijs Volkovs

Access to Online Audio
https://esmistudio.com/guitarbook2.zip

Copyright © 2024 Dmitrijs Volkovs

ISBN: 978-1-7637136-4-2

CONTENTS

1 Renaissance Era Composers

4 Allemande *(Anonymous)*
5 Balletto *(Anonymous)*
6 Galliarde *(Anonymous)*
7 Pavane *(Anonymous)*
8 Air *(Thomas Robinson)*
10 Galliard *(Emmanuel Adriaenssen)*
13 Wilson's_Wilde *(Anonymous)*
15 Alman *(Robert Johnson)*
17 Pavane I *(Luys Milan)*
19 My Lord Willoughby's Welcome Home *(John Dowland)*

24 Baroque Era Composers

26 Entree *(Giuseppe Antonio Brescianello)*
28 Preludium *(Robert de Visee)*
30 Allemande *(Robert de Visee)*
32 Sarabande *(Robert de Visee)*
34 Gigue *(Robert de Visee)*
36 Bourree *(Silvius Leopold Weiss)*
39 Sarabande *(Silvius Leopold Weiss)*
41 Menuet *(Silvius Leopold Weiss)*
42 Menuet II *(Silvius Leopold Weiss)*
43 Bouree *(Johann Sebastian Bach)*
45 Gavotte *(Johann Sebastian Bach)*
49 Sarabande *(Johann Sebastian Bach)*
50 Preludium *(Johann Sebastian Bach)*

54 Classical Era Composers

56 Andantino *(Mauro Giuliani)*
58 Andantino 2 *(Mauro Giuliani)*
60 Andante *(Fernando Sor)*
62 Etude n 17 *(Fernando Sor)*
64 Etude n 22 *(Fernando Sor)*
66 Allegretto *(Dionisio Aguado)*
68 Waltz *(Dionisio Aguado)*
70 Waltz *(Fernando Sor)*
71 Menuet *(Fernando Sor)*

73 Romantic Era Composers

76 Barcarolle *(Napoleon Coste)*
77 Etude *(Napoleon Coste)*
79 Waltz *(Napoleon Coste)*
82 Etude N 1 *(Francisco Tarrega)*
84 Adelita *(Francisco Tarrega)*
85 Etude N 3 *(Mateo Carcassi)*
87 Etude N 16 *(Mateo Carcassi)*
89 Nocturne *(Johann Kaspar Mertz)*
91 Ejercicio *(Jose Ferrer)*
93 Tango N 3 *(Jose Ferrer)*

95 Latin America/Traditional

96 Greensleeves *(Traditional)*
98 Choro *(Domingos Semenzato)*
100 Cuban Dance *(Anonymous)*
102 Romance *(Anonymous)*
104 Choro *(Joao Pernambuco)*
106 Choro N 2 *(Joao Pernambuco)*
108 Lagrima *(Joao Pernambuco)*
111 Yolanda *(Domingos Semenzato)*

Renaissance Composers

Anonymous

The Renaissance (which means "rebirth or "revival") began around 1400 and ended in the early 1600s. The musicians and artists of the Renaissance looked back to classical models, spawning a new era of artistic growth. With the invention of the printing press, music became available to the public as never before.

Thomas Robinson (1588-1610?)

Thomas Robinson's was an English renaissance composer and music teacher, who flourished around 1600. He taught and wrote music for lute, cittern, orpharion, bandora, viol, and singing. His works for the most part consist of his own compositions.

Emmanuel Adriaenssen (1554-1604)

Emmanuel Adriaenssen was a Flemish lutenist and influential author of Pratum Musicum. This contains lute solos, and more importantly settings of madrigals for multiple lutes and different ensembles involving lutes and voices giving much study material for the researcher into renaissance performance practice. The ensemble pieces have been recorded by the Dowland Consort of Lutes.

Robert Johnson (1583-1634)

Robert Johnson was an English composer and lutenist of the late Tudor and early Jacobean eras. He is sometimes called "Robert Johnson II" to distinguish him from an earlier Scottish composer. He worked with William Shakespeare providing music for some of his later plays.

Luis de Milán (c. 1500 – c. 1561)

Luis de Milán (c. 1500 – c. 1561) was a Spanish Renaissance composer, vihuelist, and writer on music. He was the first composer in history to publish music for the vihuela de mano, an instrument employed primarily in the Iberian peninsula and some of the Italian states during the 15th and 16th centuries, and he was also one of the first musicians to specify verbal tempo indications in his music.

John Dowland (1563-1626)

John Dowland was an English Renaissance composer, lutenist, and singer. He is best known today for his melancholy songs such as "Come, heavy sleep", "Come again", "Flow my tears", "I saw my Lady weepe" and "In darkness let me dwell", but his instrumental music has undergone a major revival, and with the 20th century's early music revival, has been a continuing source of repertoire for lutenists and classical guitarists.

Allemande

Anonymous XVI century

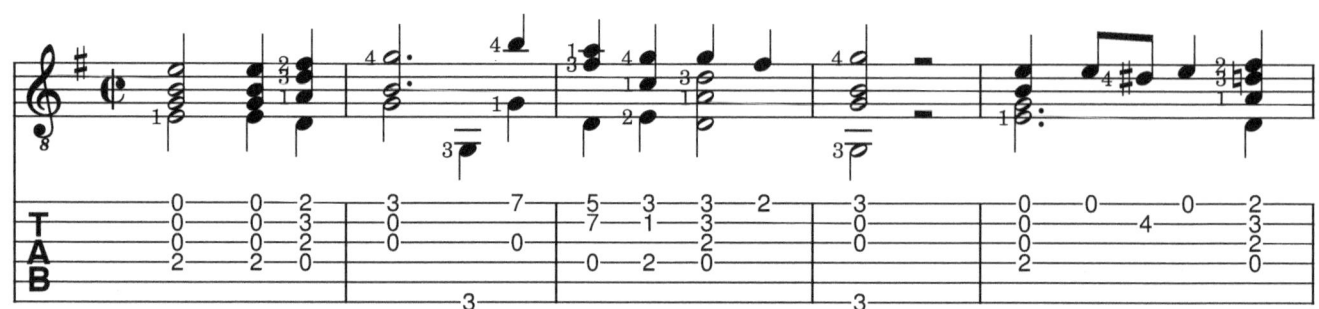

Balletto

Anonymous XVI century

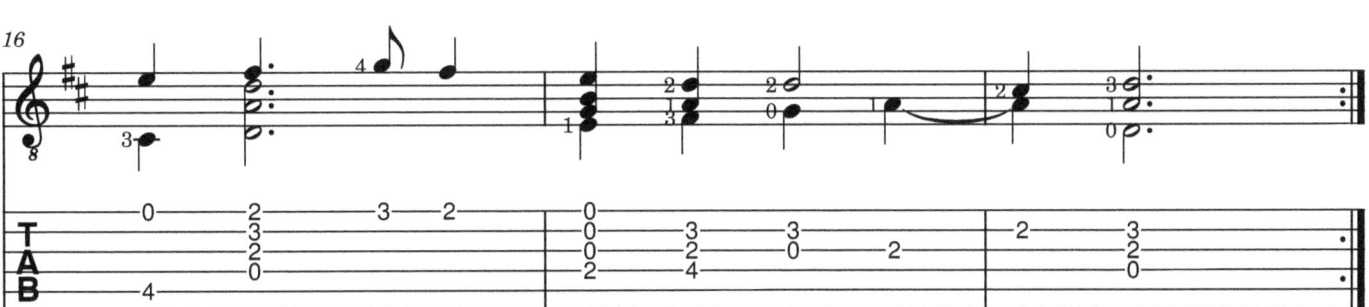

Galliarde

Anonymous XVI century

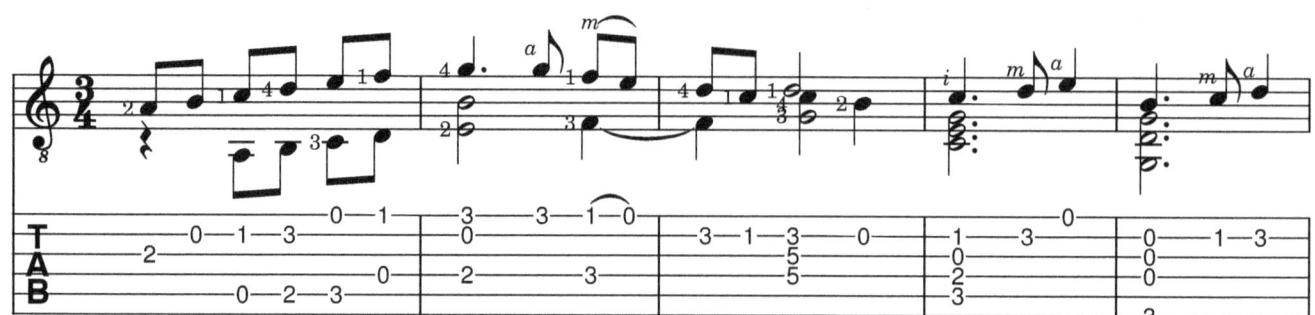

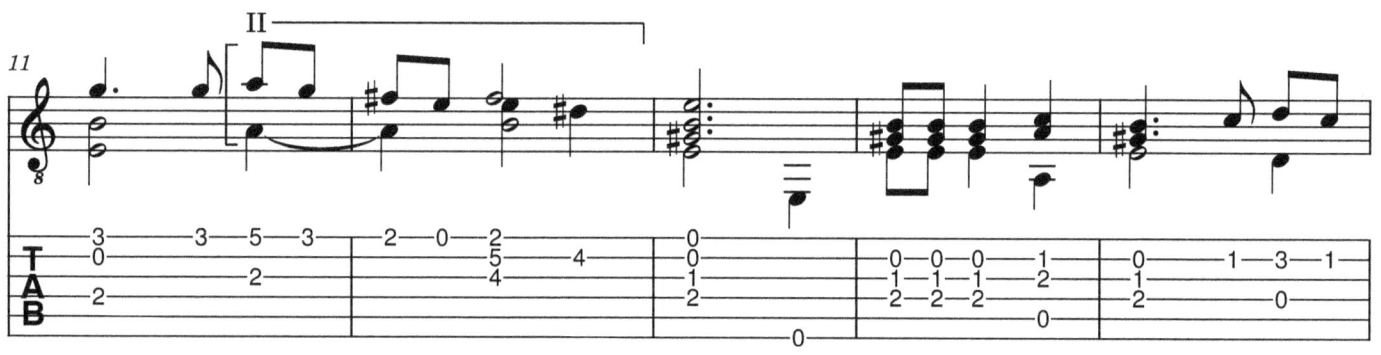

Pavane

Anonymous XVI century

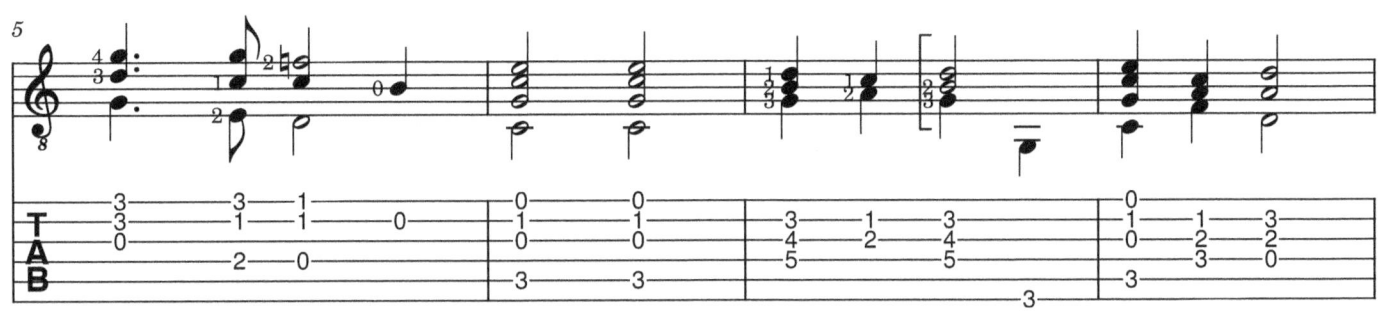

AIR

Thomas Robinson (1560-1610)

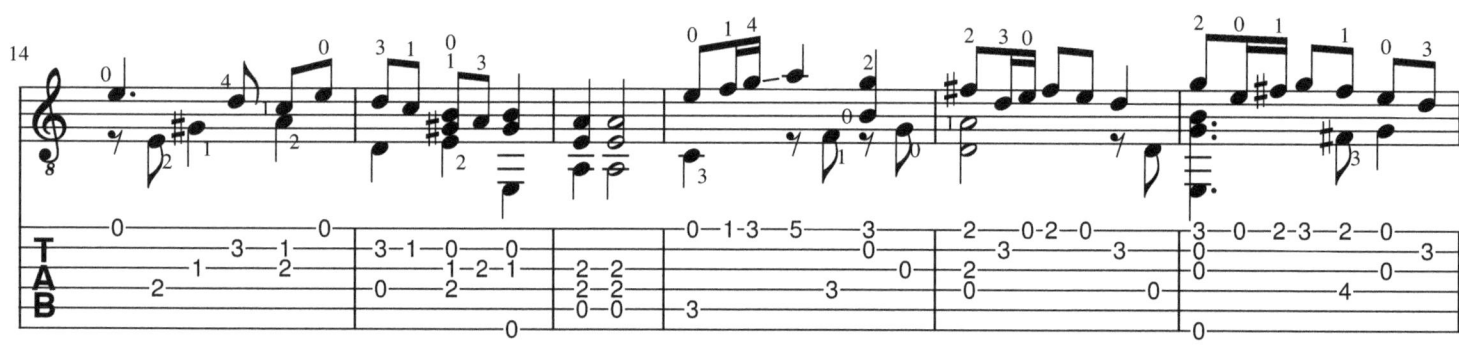

Galliard

Emmanuel Adriaenssen (1550-1604)

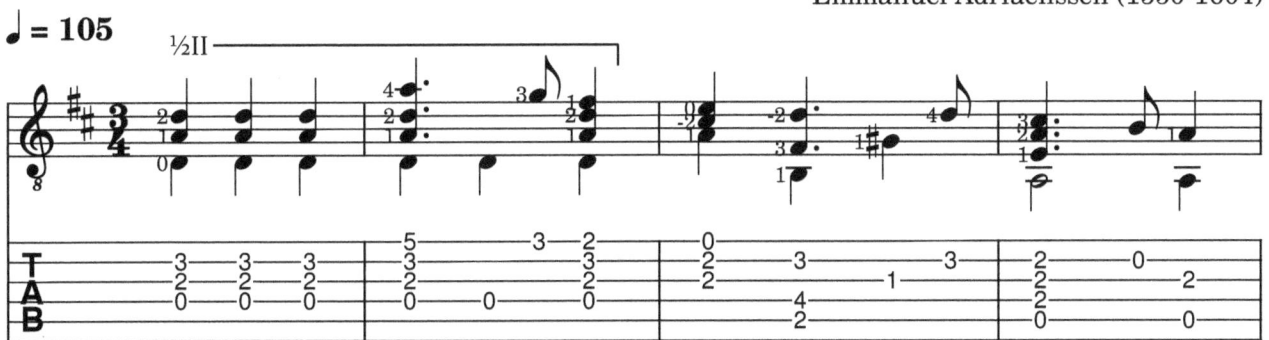

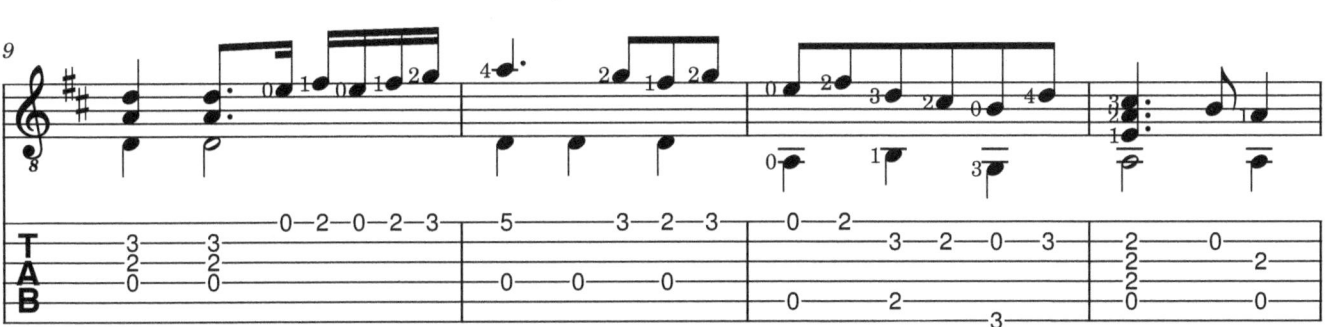

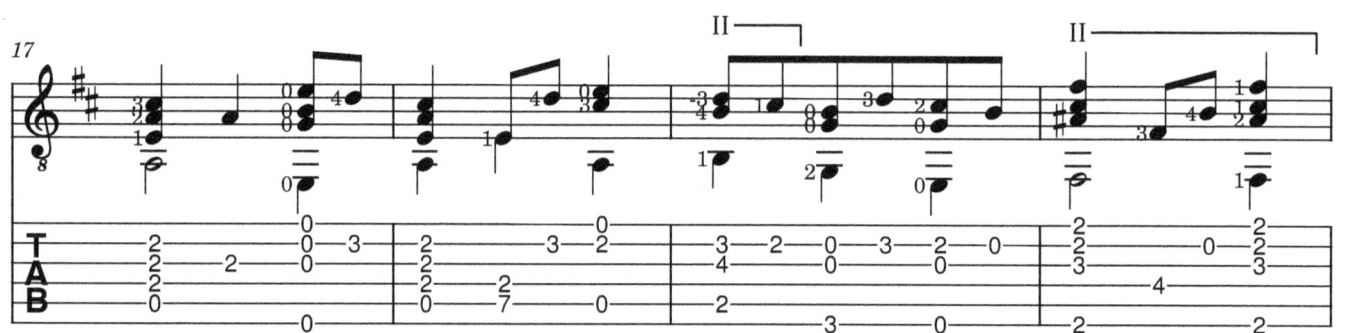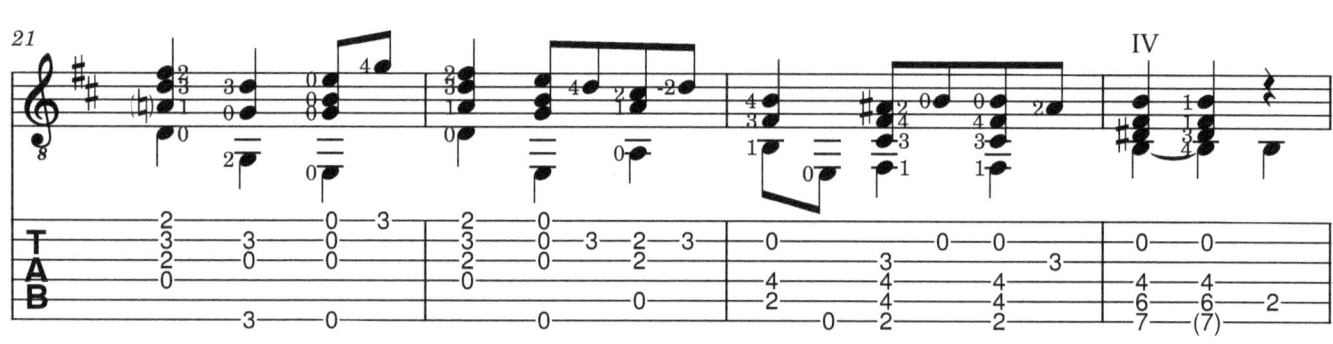

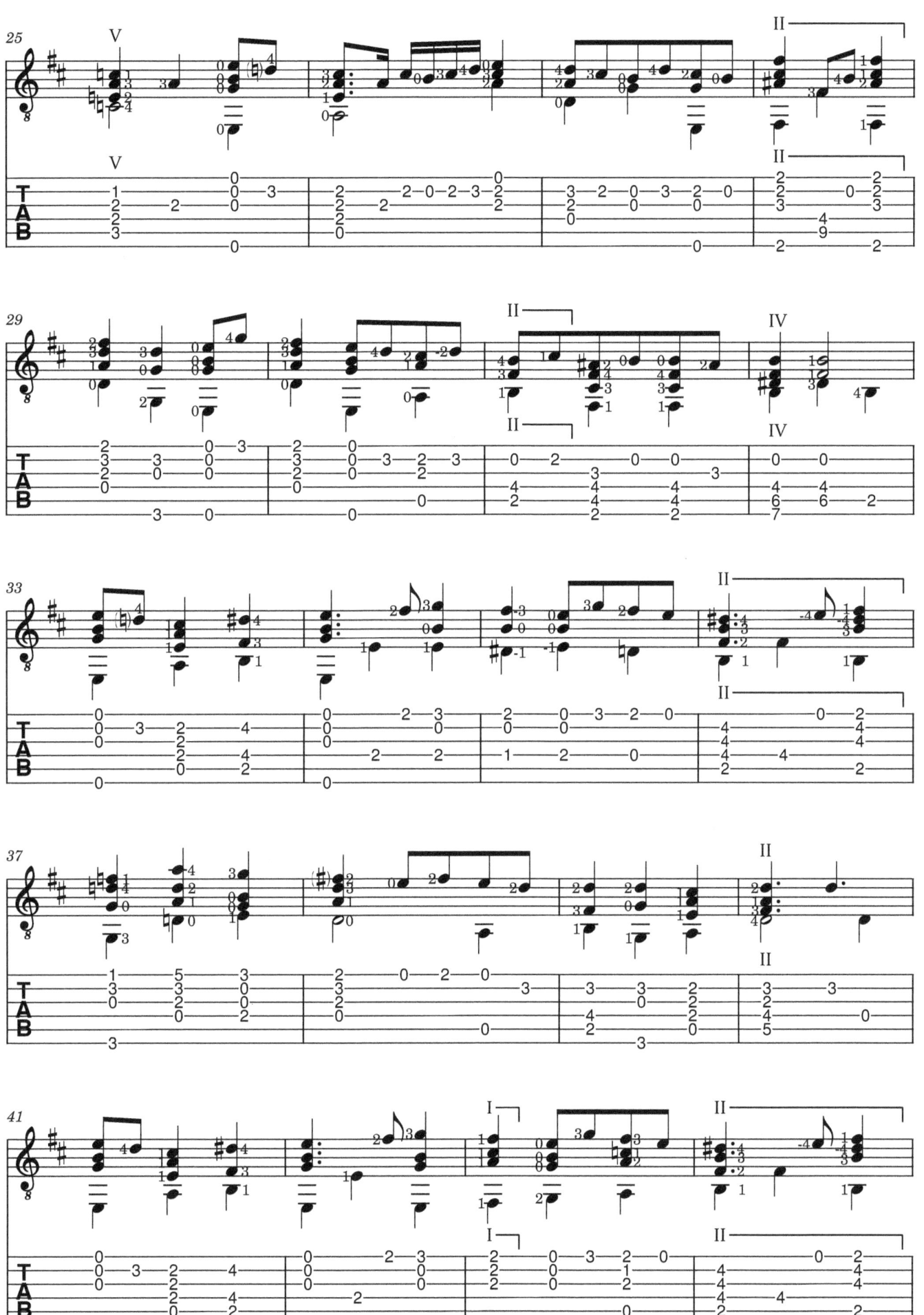

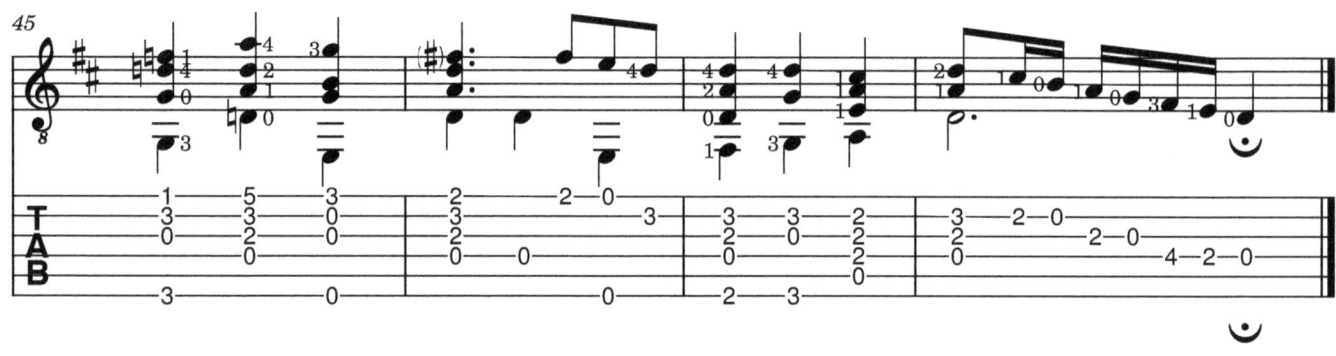

Wilson's Wilde

Anonymous XVI century

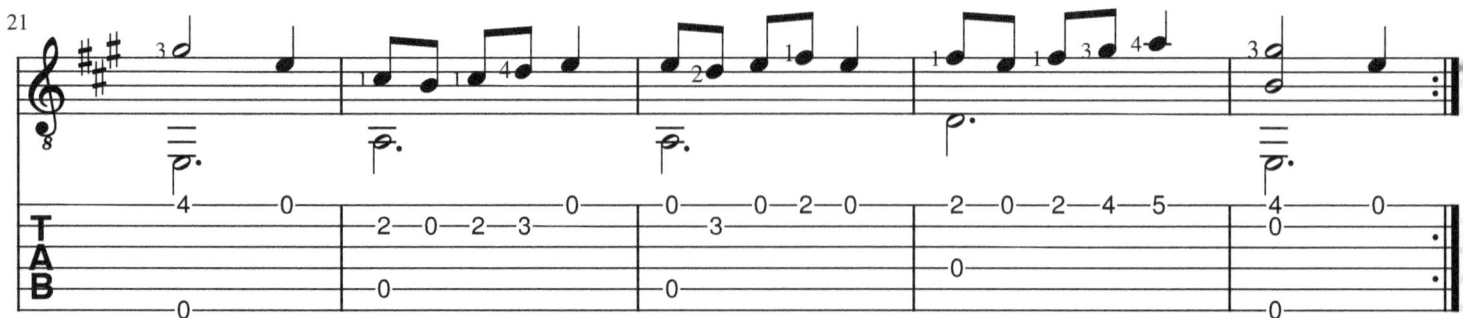
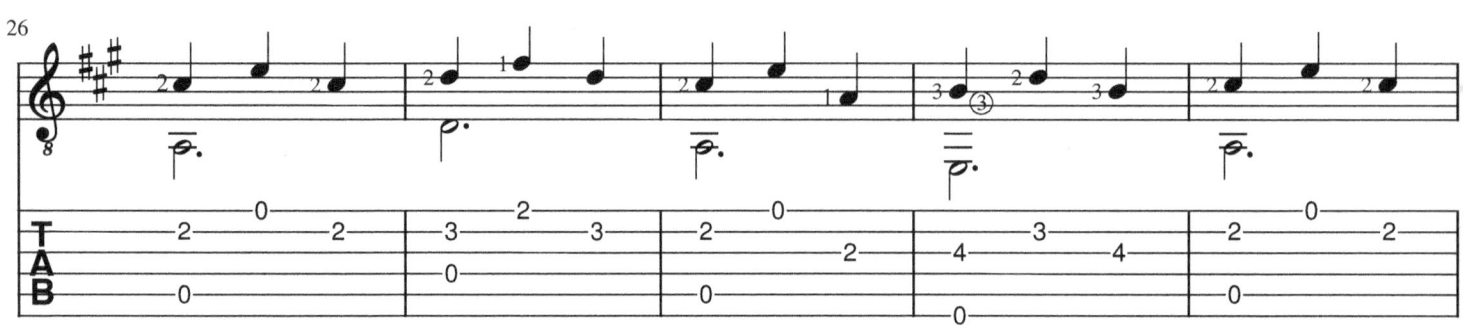

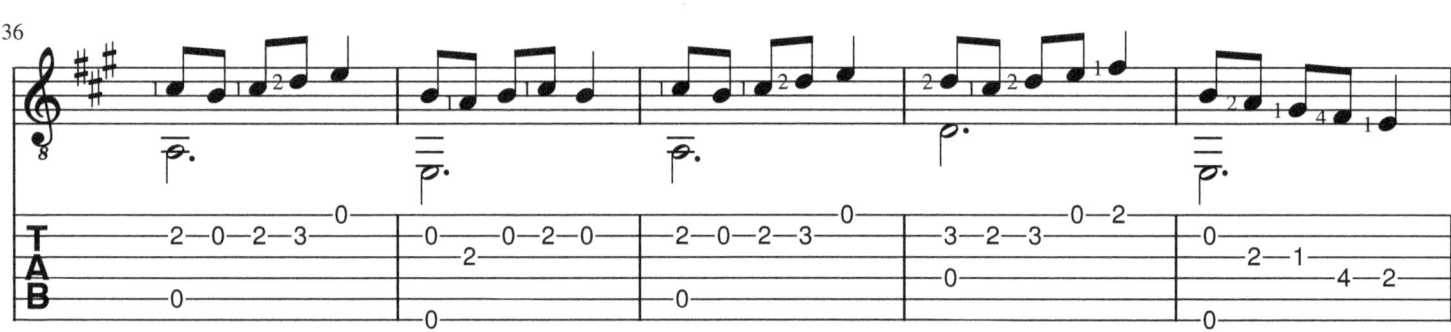

Alman

Robert Johnson (1583-1633)

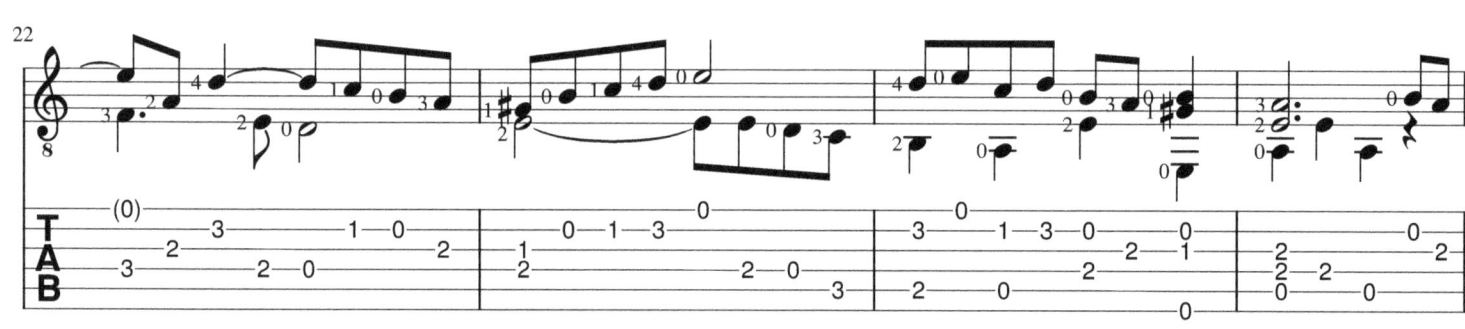
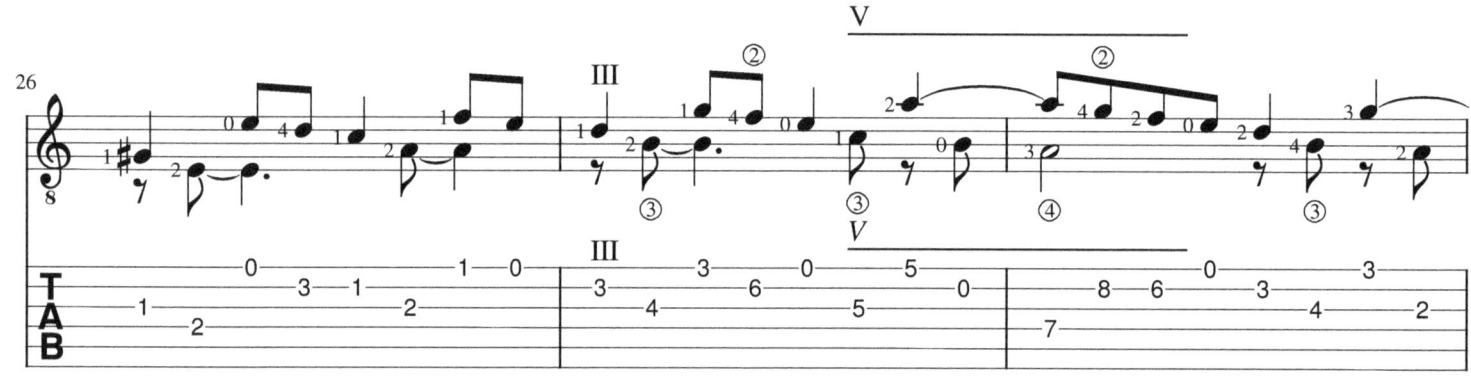

Pavane I

Luys Milán (1500 - 1562)

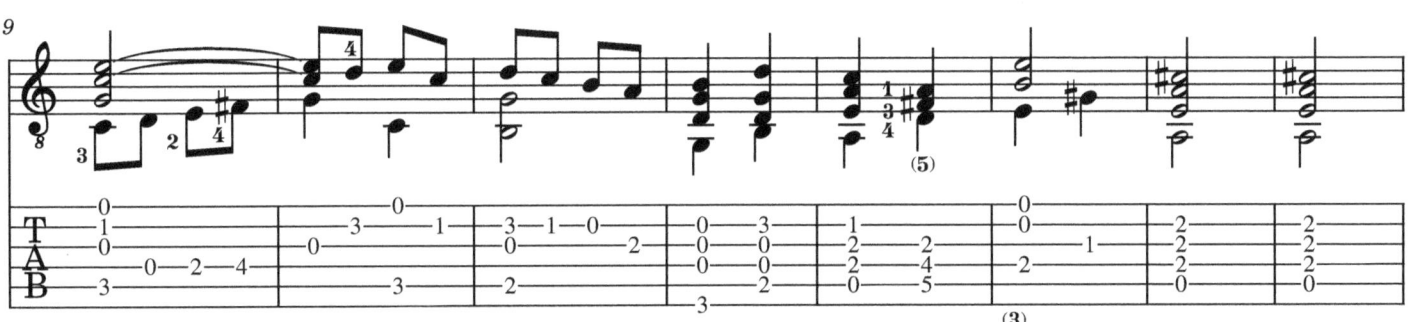
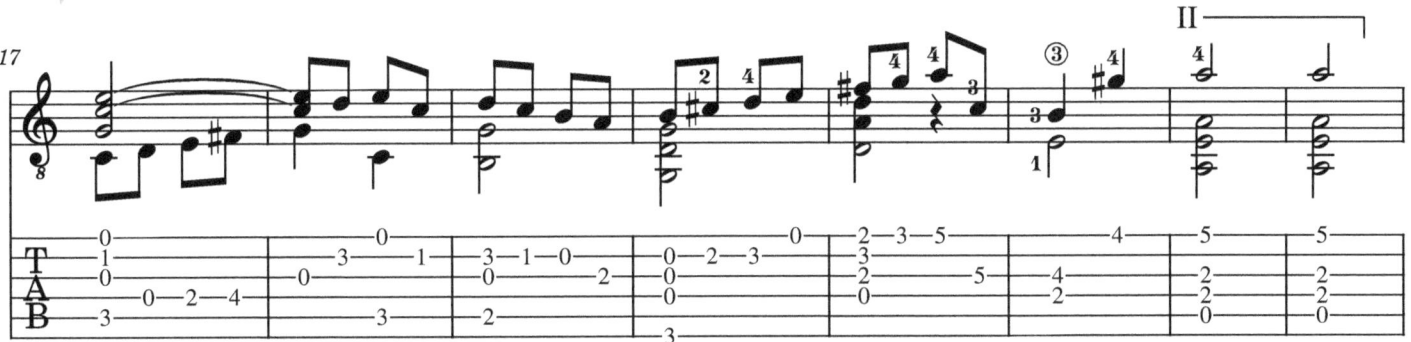

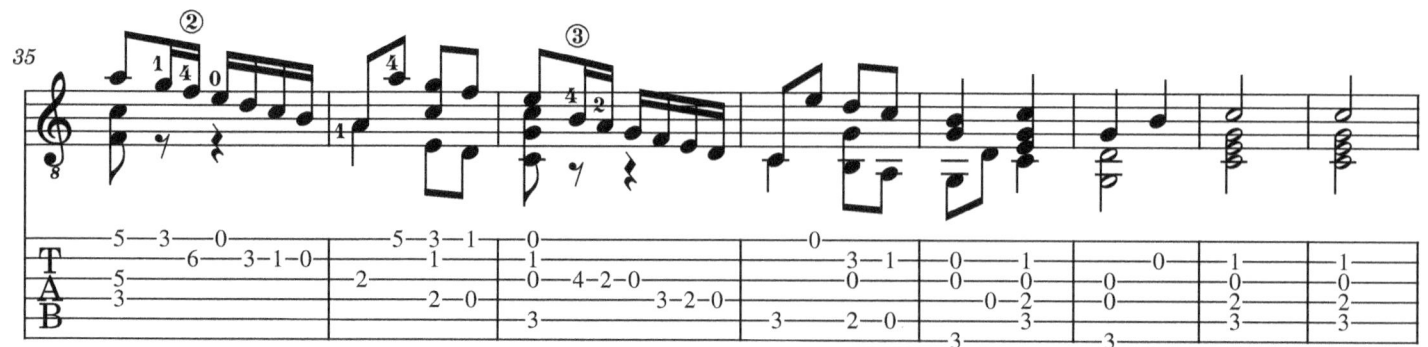

My Lord Willoughby's Welcome Home

John Dowland (1563-1626)

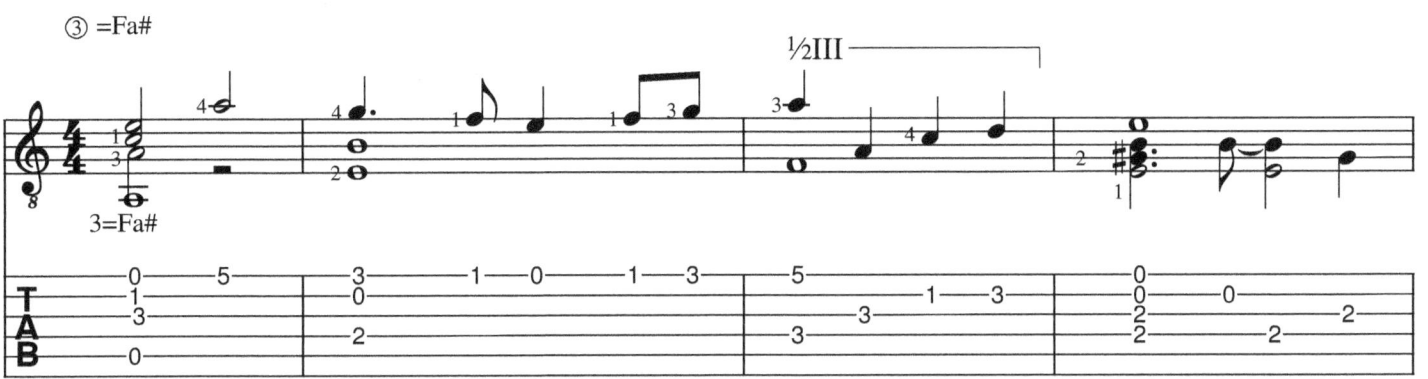

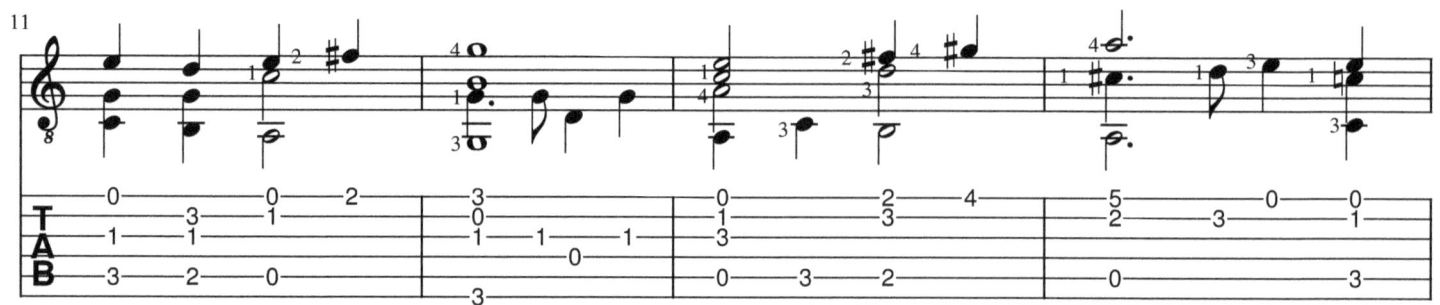

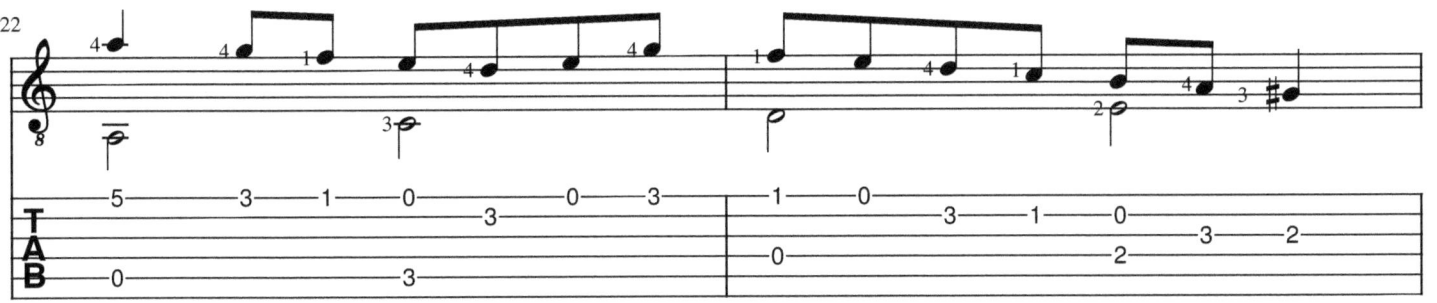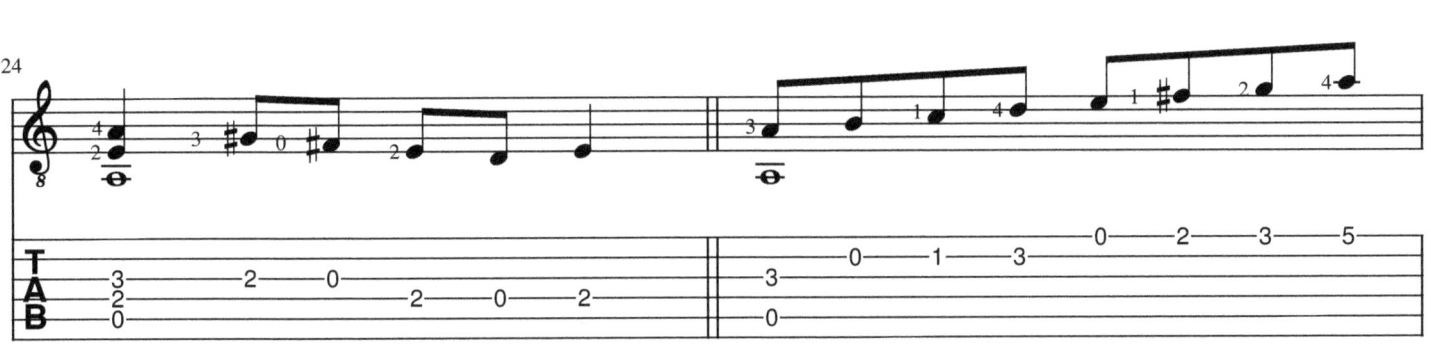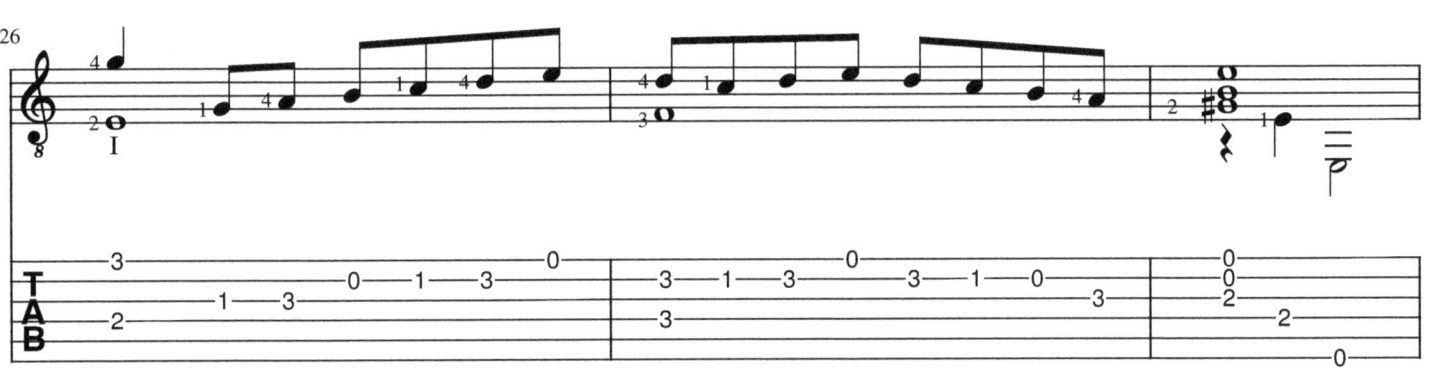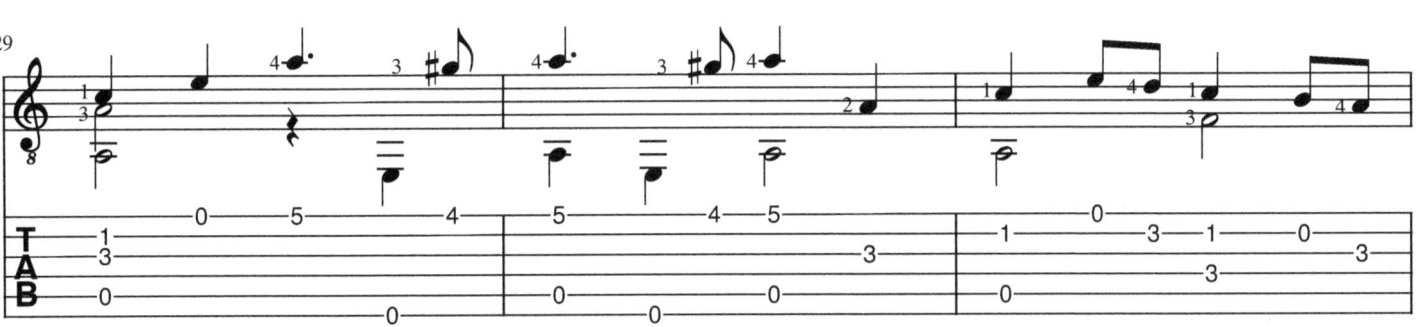

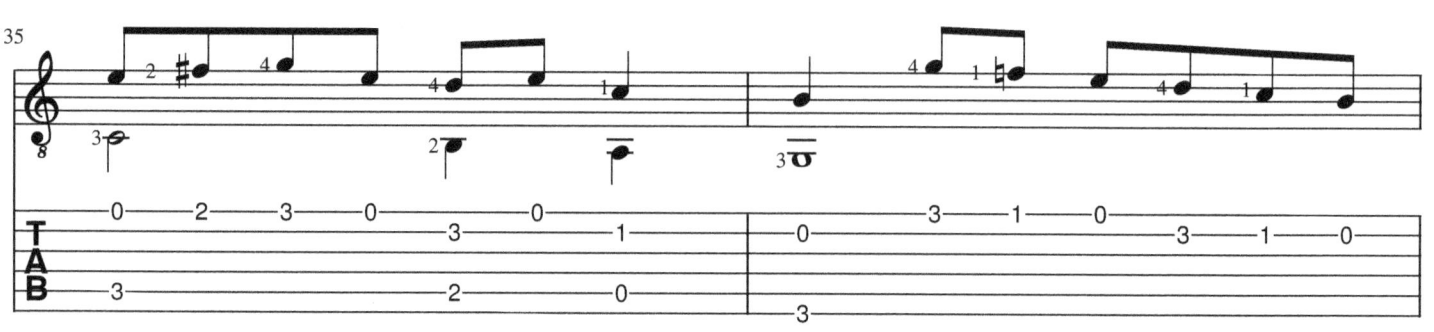
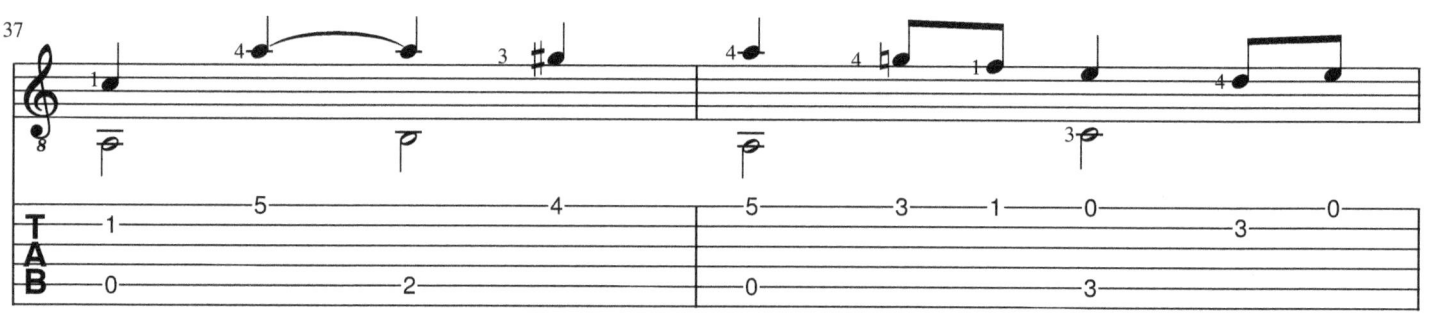

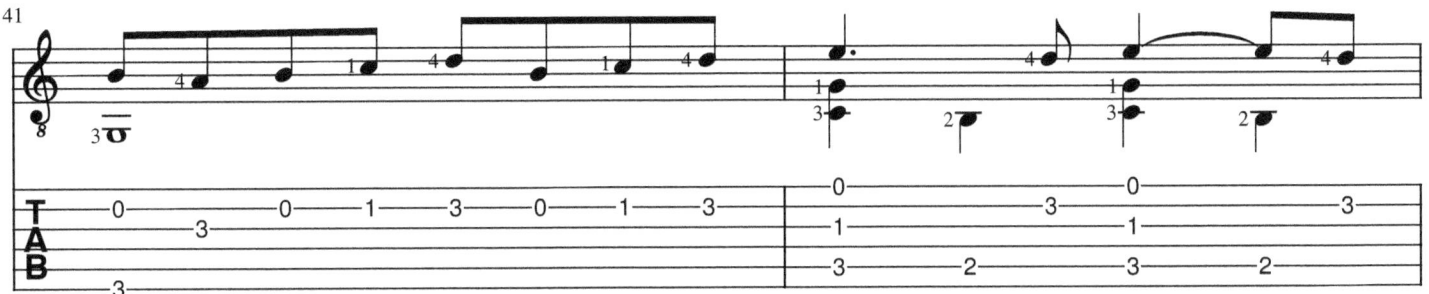

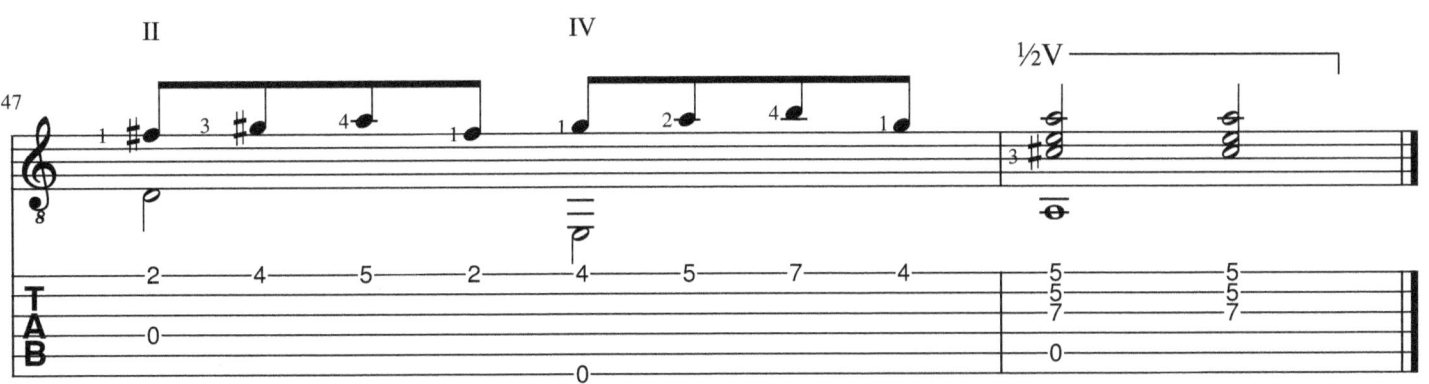

Baroque Composers

Giuseppe Antonio Brescianello (1690-1758)

Giuseppe Antonio Brescianello was an Italian Baroque composer and violinist. He invigorated musical life in Stuttgart. His contemporaries praised his chamber works. The music of Brescianello shows great sense of melody, profound harmonic imagination combined with strong rhythmic element so typical to Italian school of the time.

Robert de Visee (1655 – 1732)

Robert de Visée was a lutenist, guitarist, theorbist and viol player at the court of Louis XIV, as well as a singer, and composer for lute, theorbo and guitar. Robert de Visée's origin is unknown, although a Portuguese origin of his surname had been suggested. Visée published two books of guitar music which contained twelve suites between them, as well as a few isolated pieces.

Silvius Leopold Weiss (1687-1750)

Silvius Leopold Weiss was a German composer and lutenist. Weiss was one of the most important and most prolific composers of lute music in history and one of the best-known and most technically accomplished lutenists of his day. He wrote around 600 pieces for lute, most of them grouped into 'sonatas' or suites, which consist mostly of baroque dance pieces.

Johann Sebastian Bach (1685-1750)

Johann Sebastian Bach was a German composer, organist, harpsichordist, violist, and violinist whose sacred and secular works for choir, orchestra, and solo instruments drew together the strands of the Baroque period and brought it to its ultimate maturity.

Entrée

Giuseppe Antonio Brescianello (1690-1758)

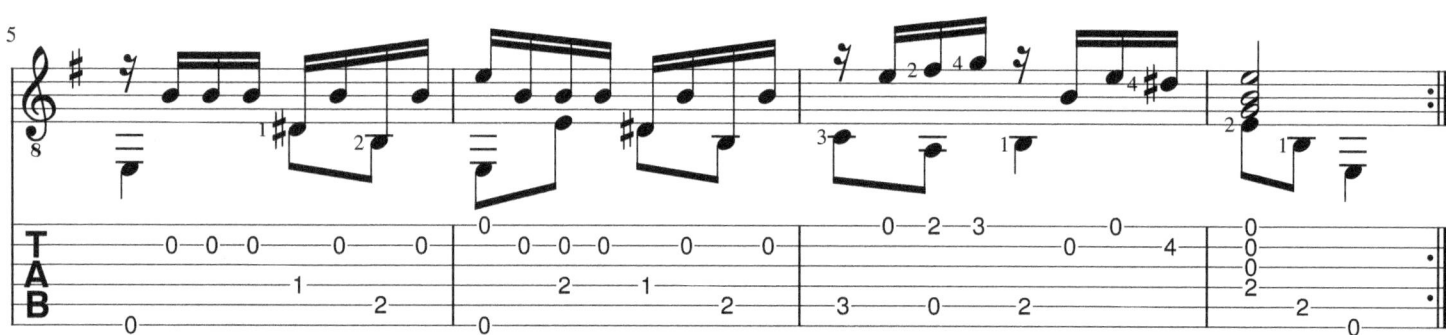
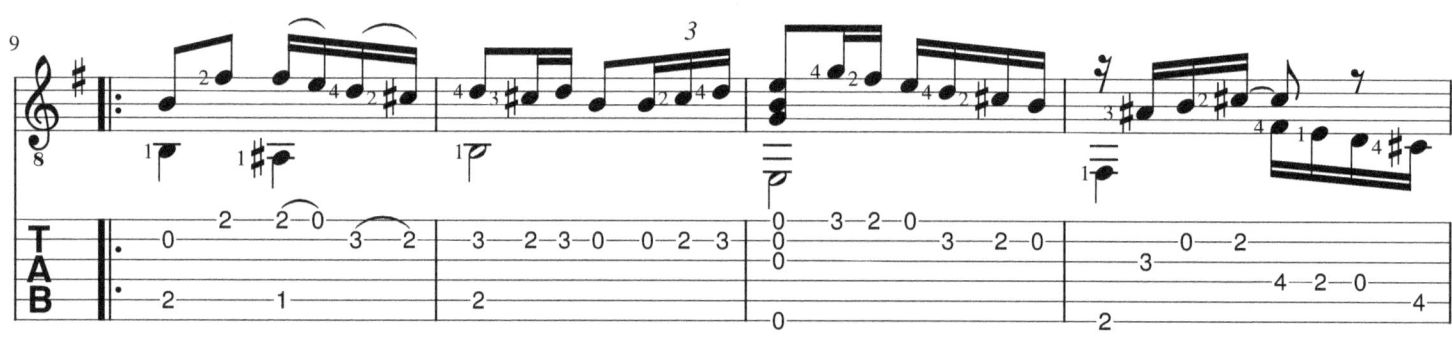

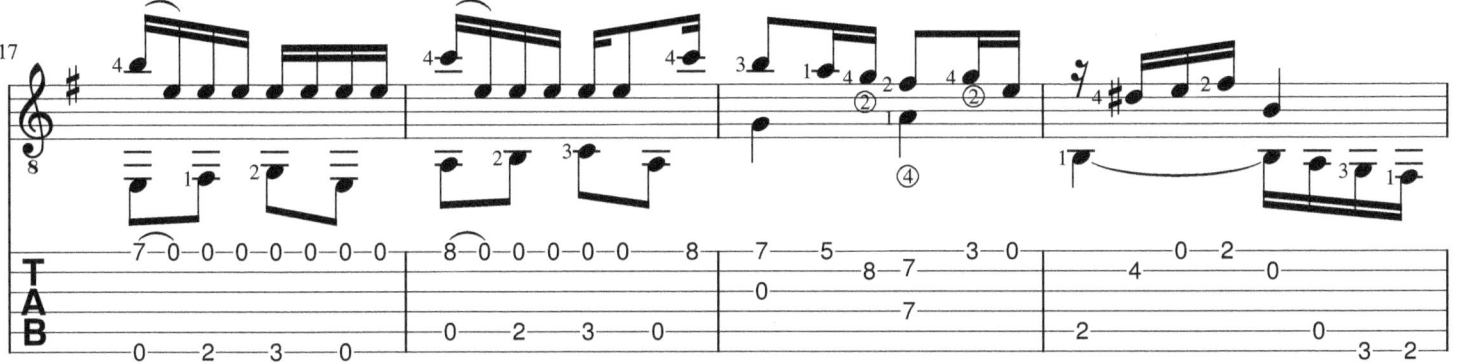
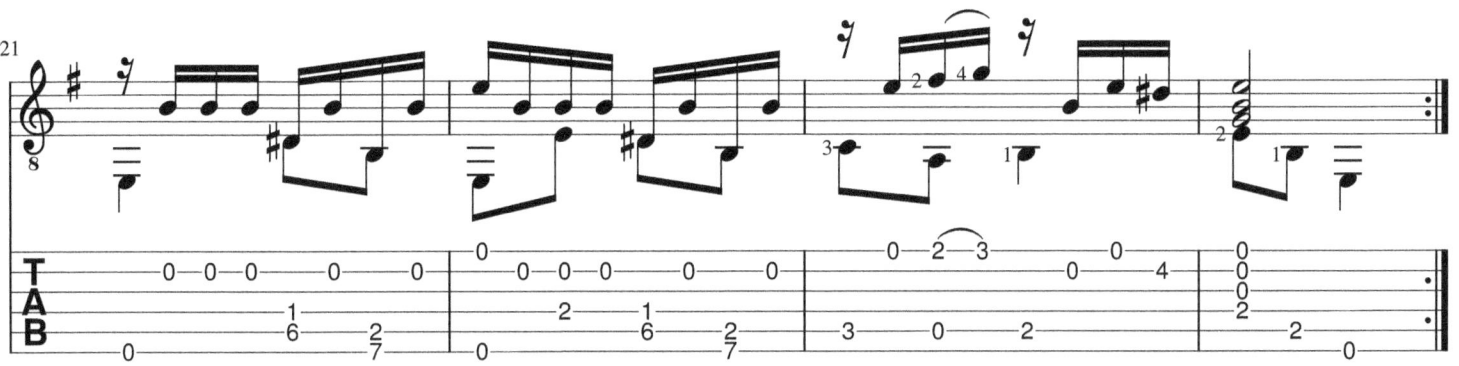

Preludium

Robert de Visée (1650-1725)

Allemande

Robert de Visée (1650-1725)

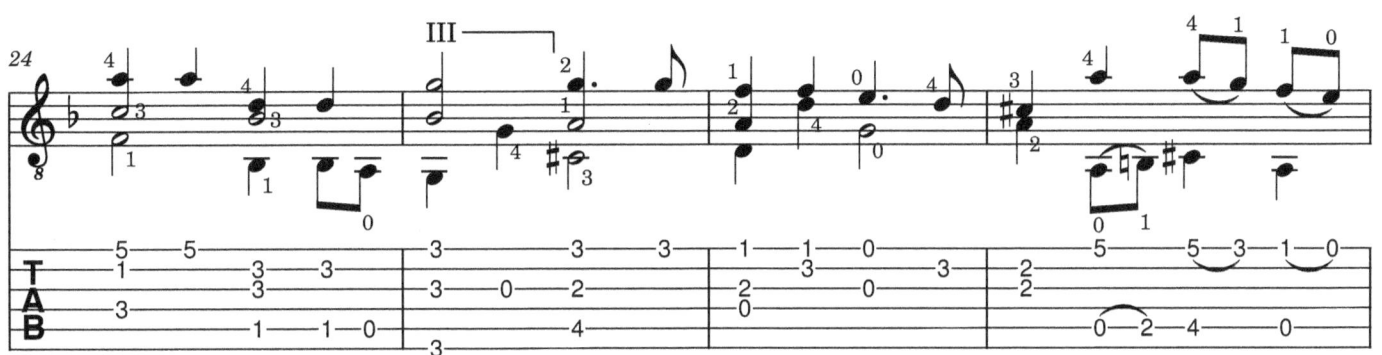
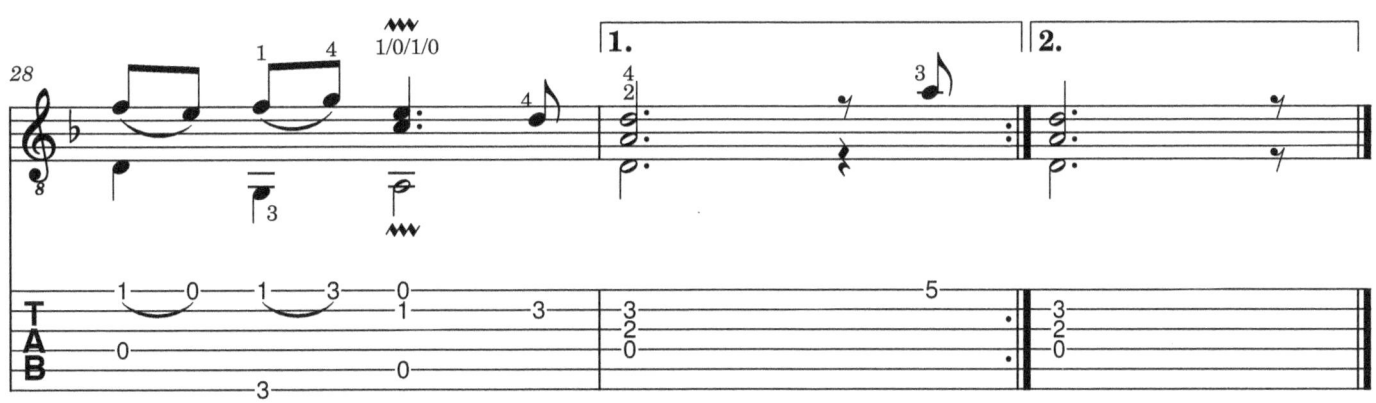

Sarabande

Robert de Visée (1650-1725)

Gigue

Robert de Visée (1650-1725)

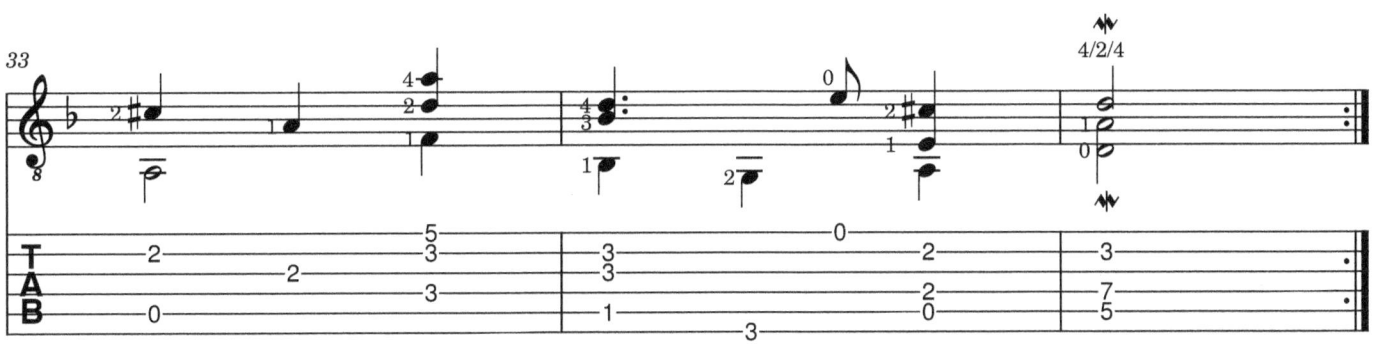

Bourree

Silvius Leopold Weiss (1687-1750)

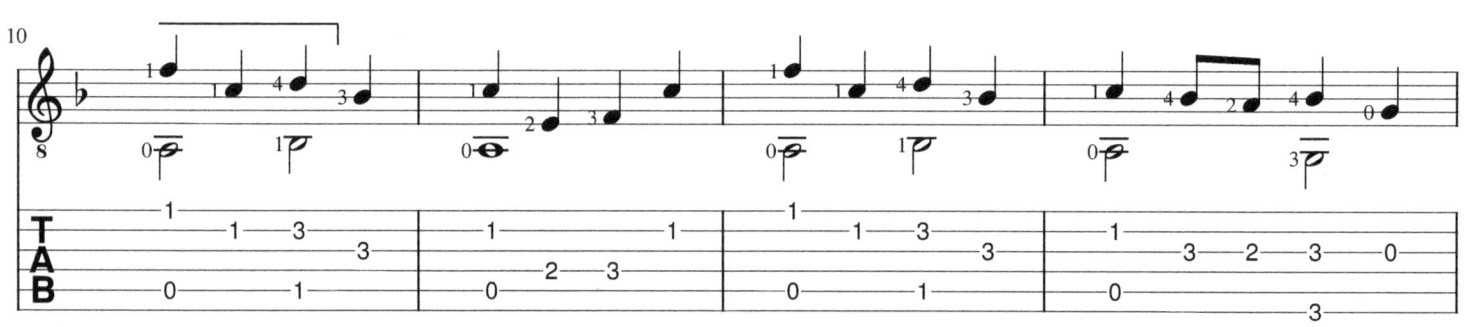
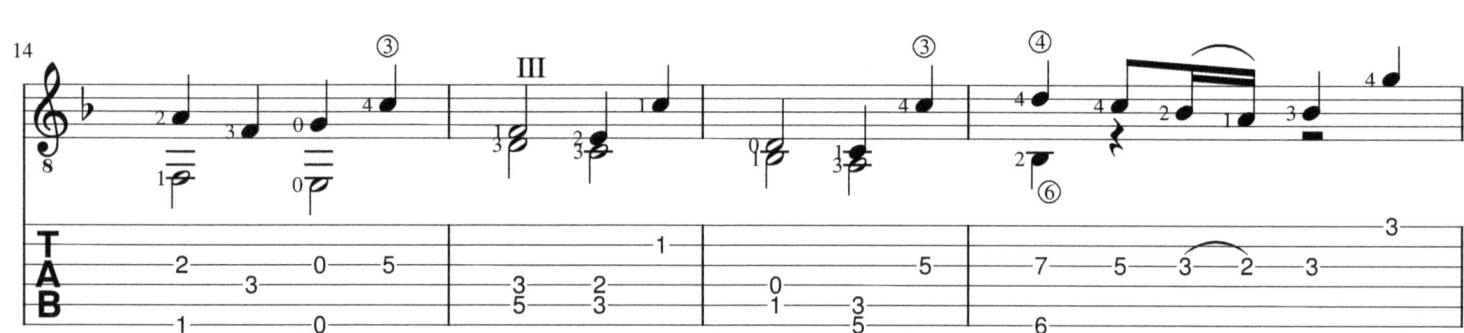

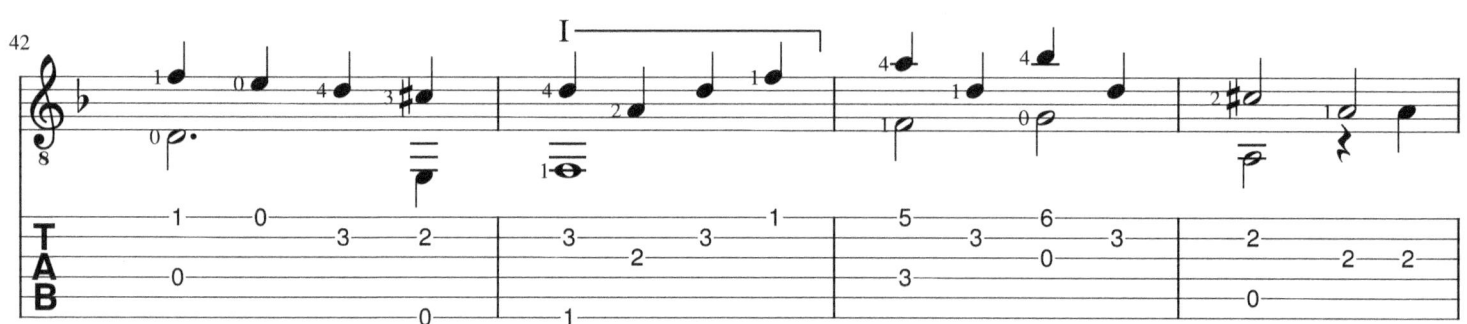
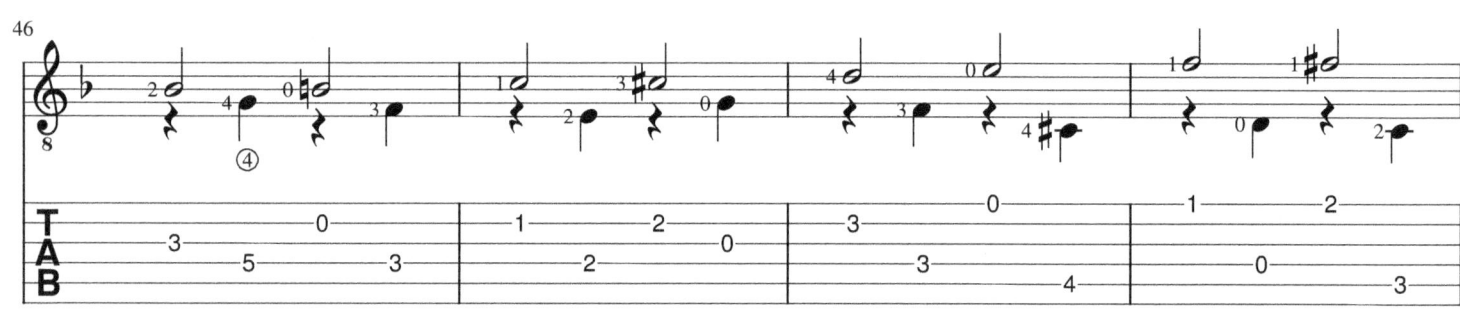
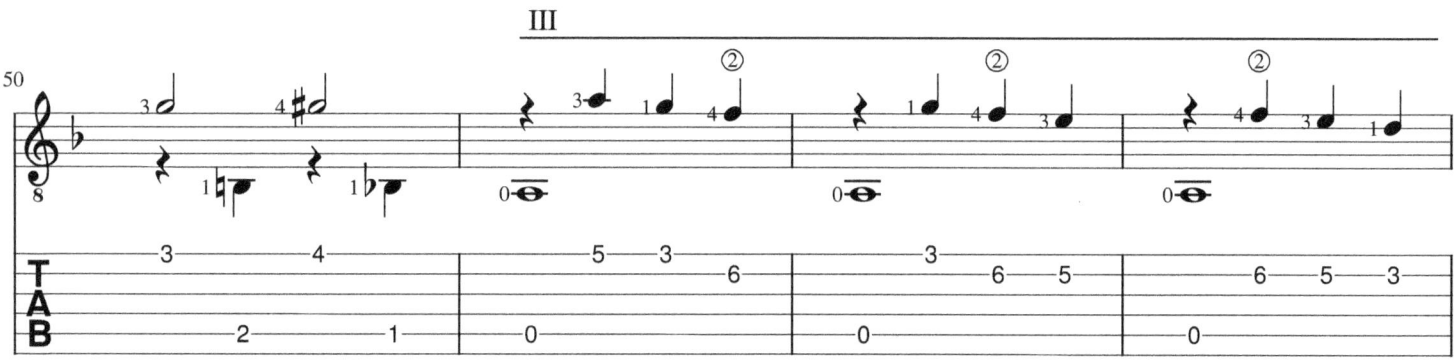
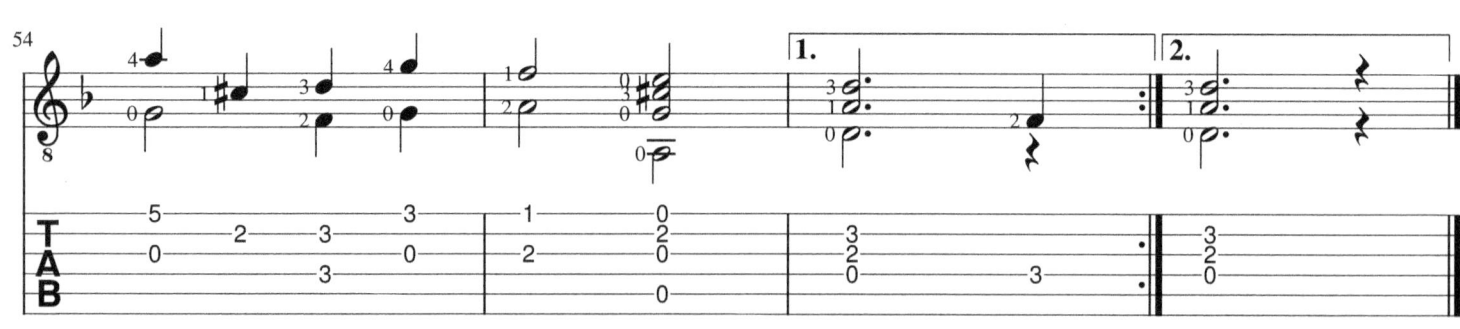

Sarabande

Silvius Leopold Weiss (1687-1750)

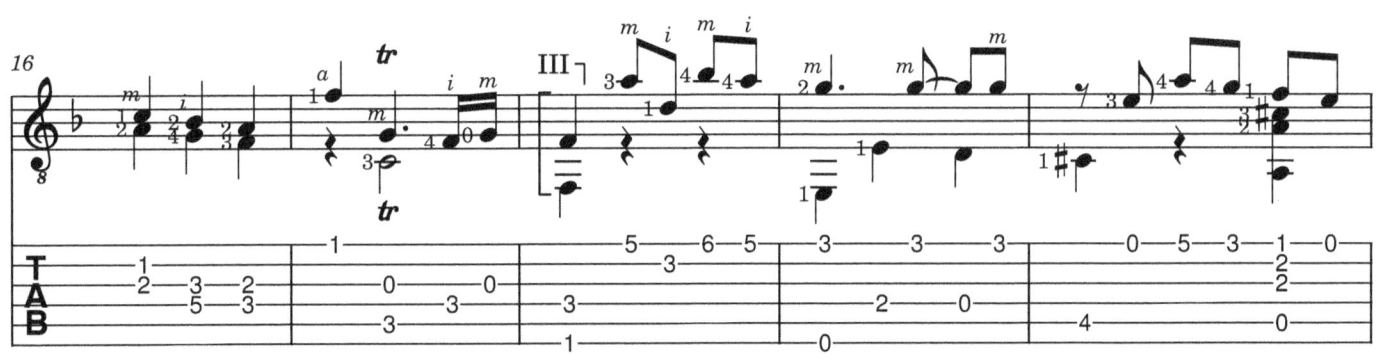

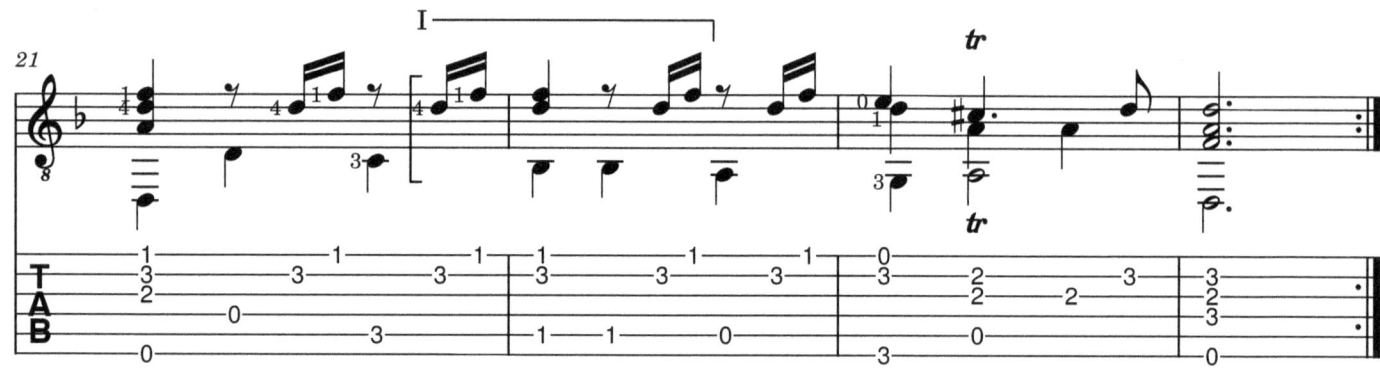

Menuet

Silvius Leopold Weiss (1687-1750)

Menuet II

Silvius Leopold Weiss (1687-1750)

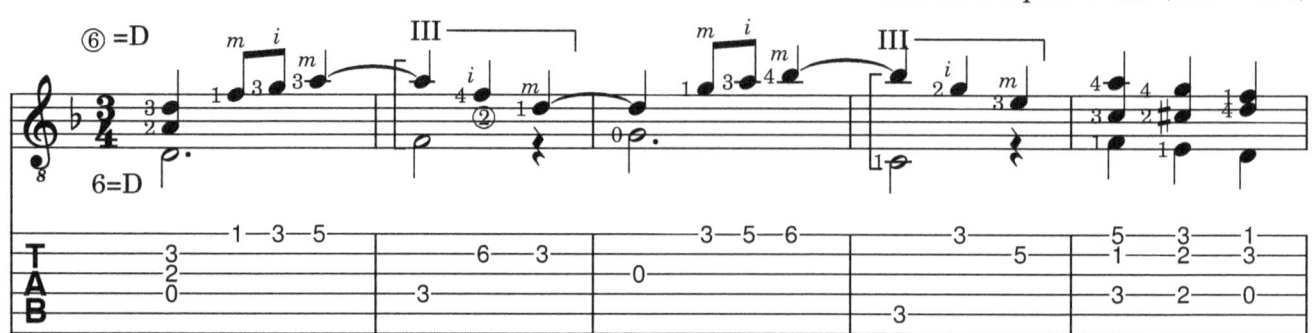
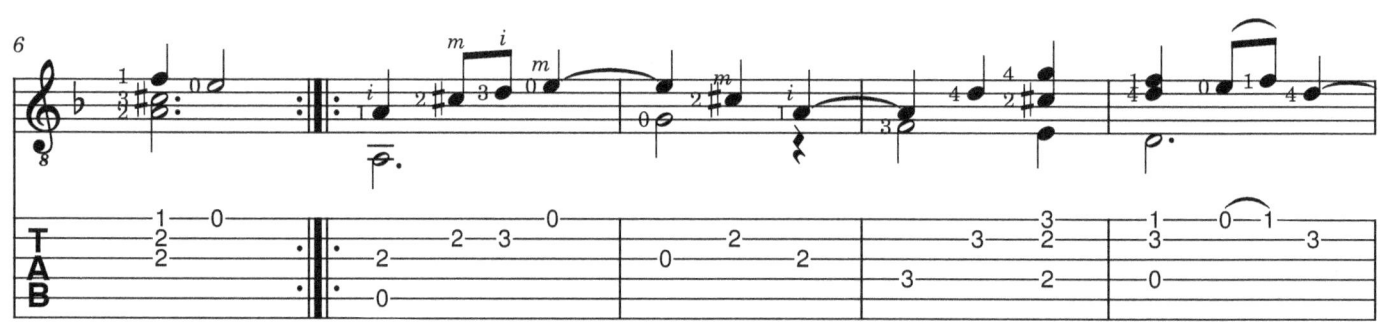
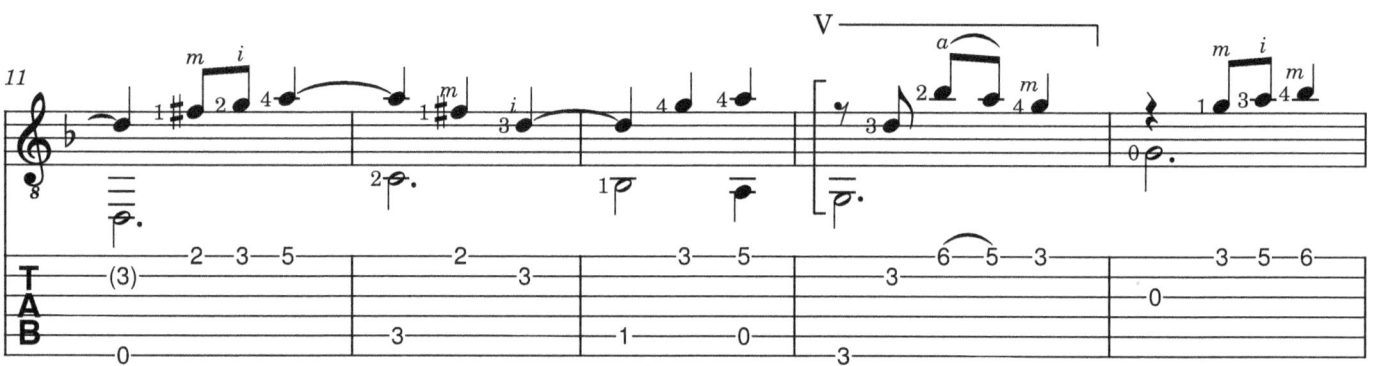
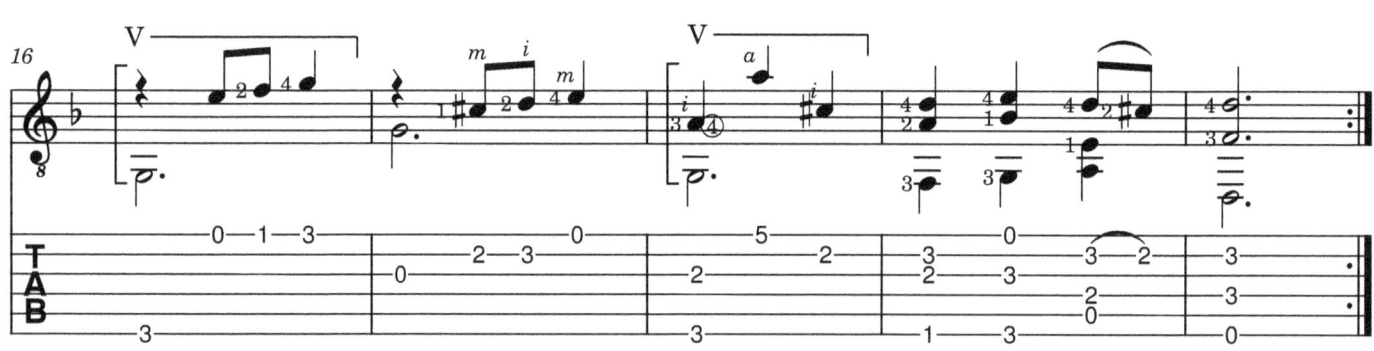

Bouree

Johann Sebastian Bach (1685-1750)

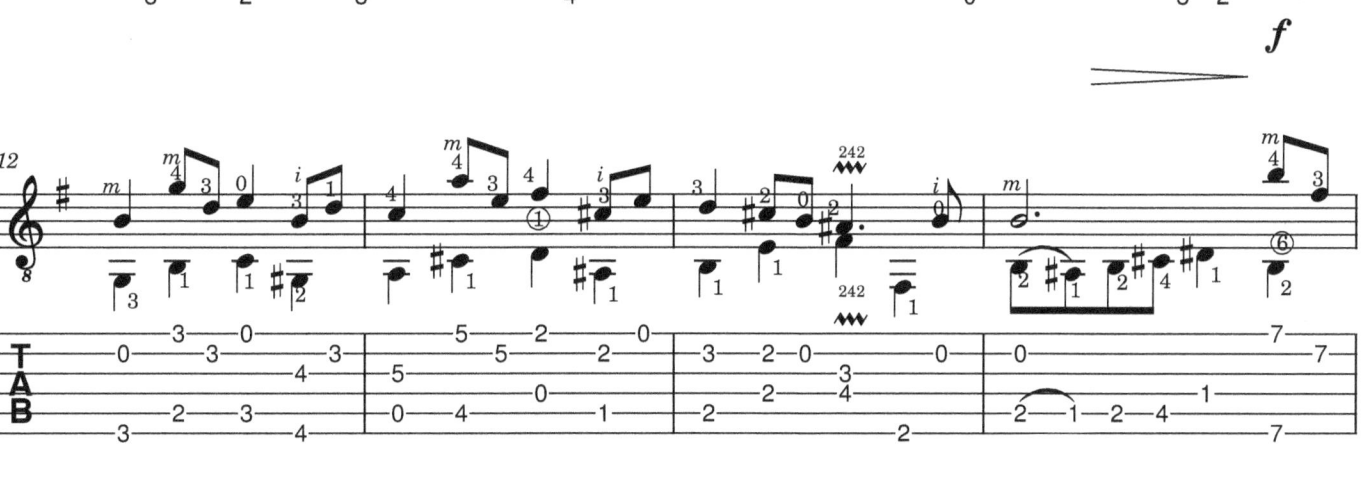

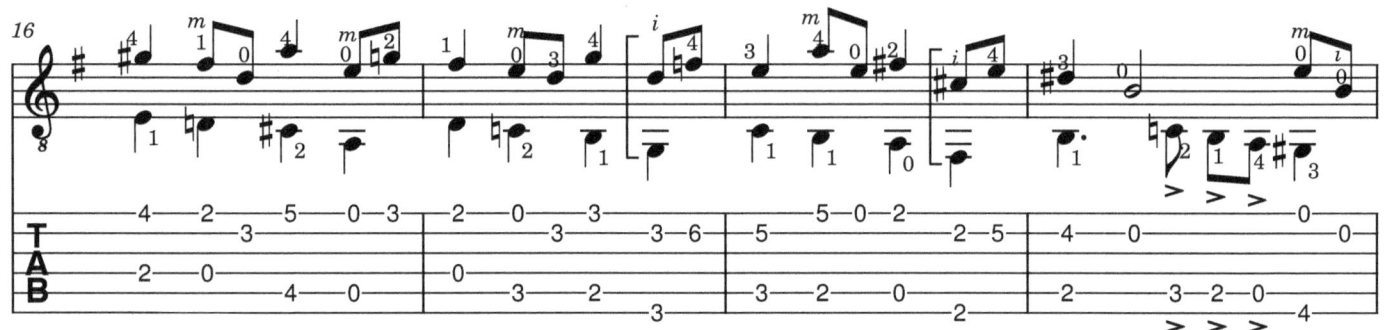
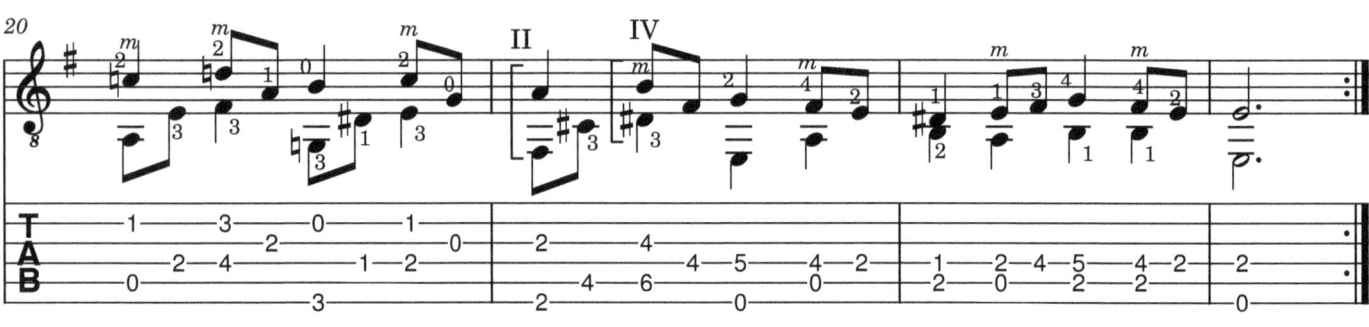

Gavotte (from suite 6 for cello, BWV 1012)

Johann Sebastian Bach (1685-1750)

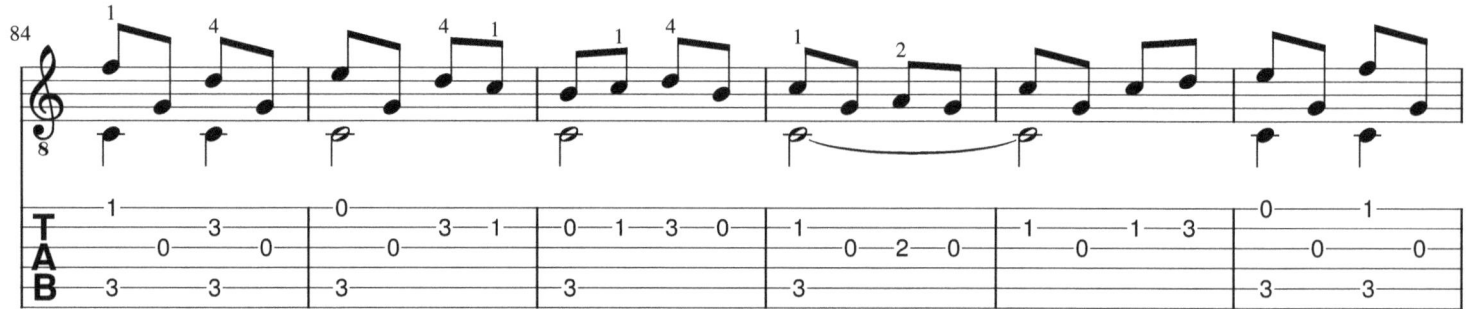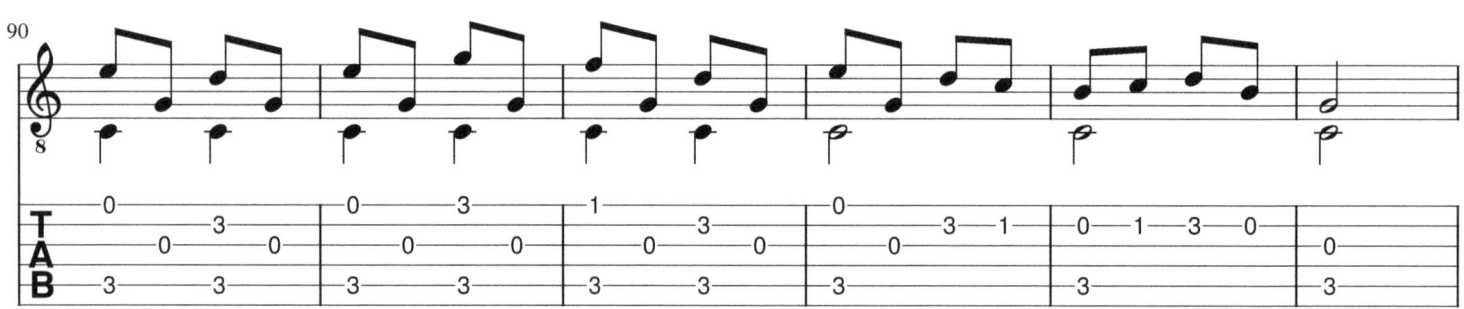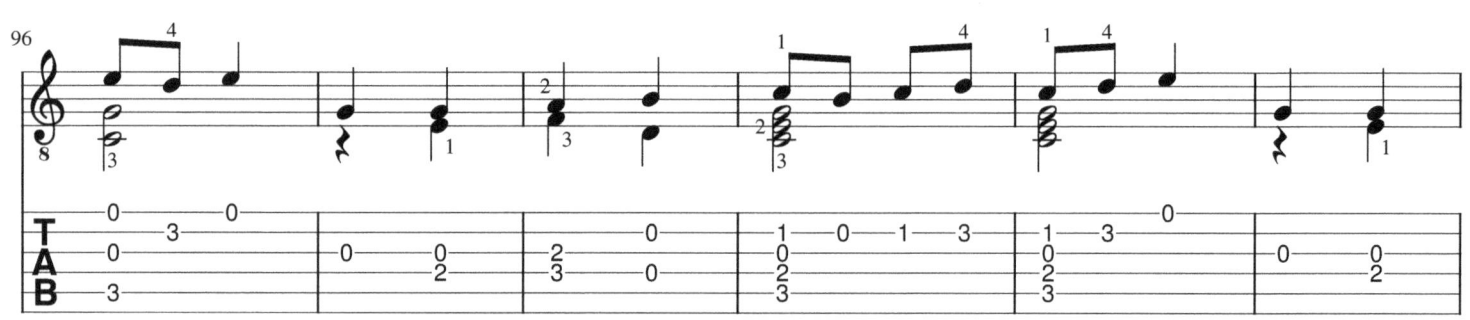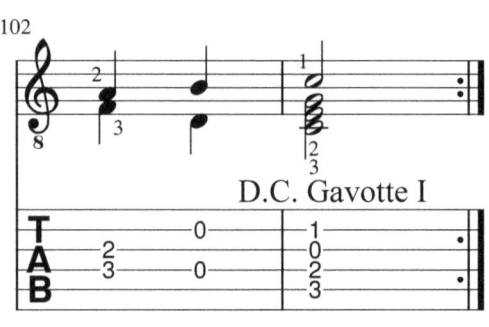

D.C. Gavotte I

Sarabande

Johann Sebastian Bach (1685-1750)

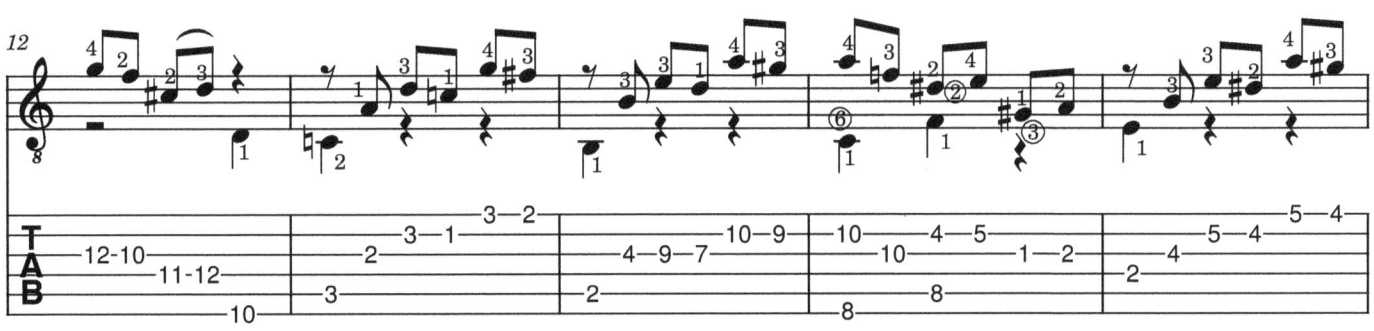
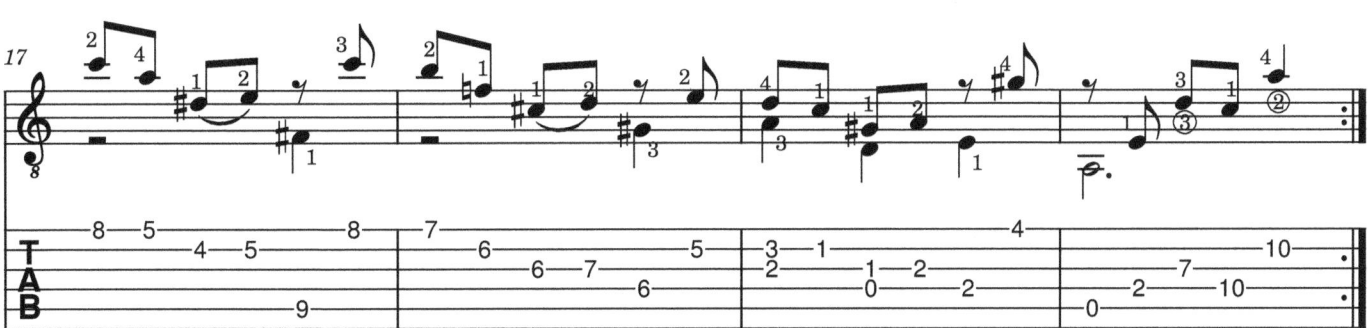

Preludium

Johann Sebastian Bach (1685-1750)

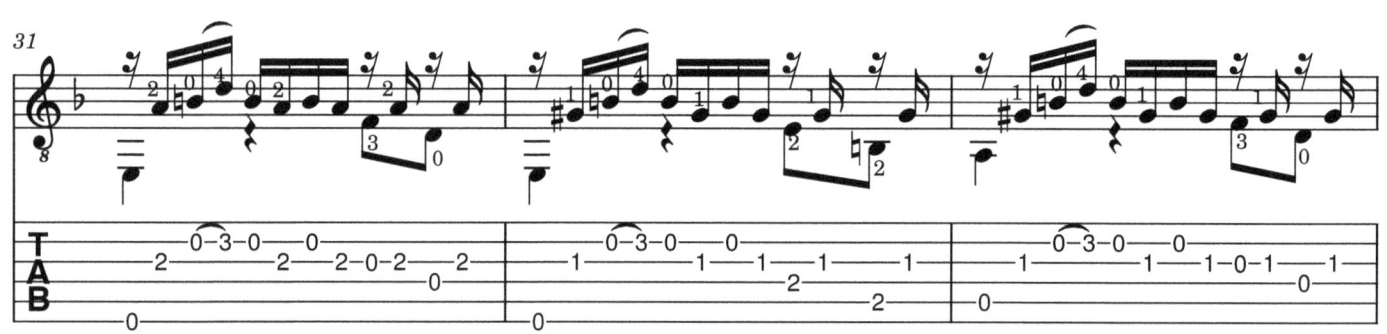
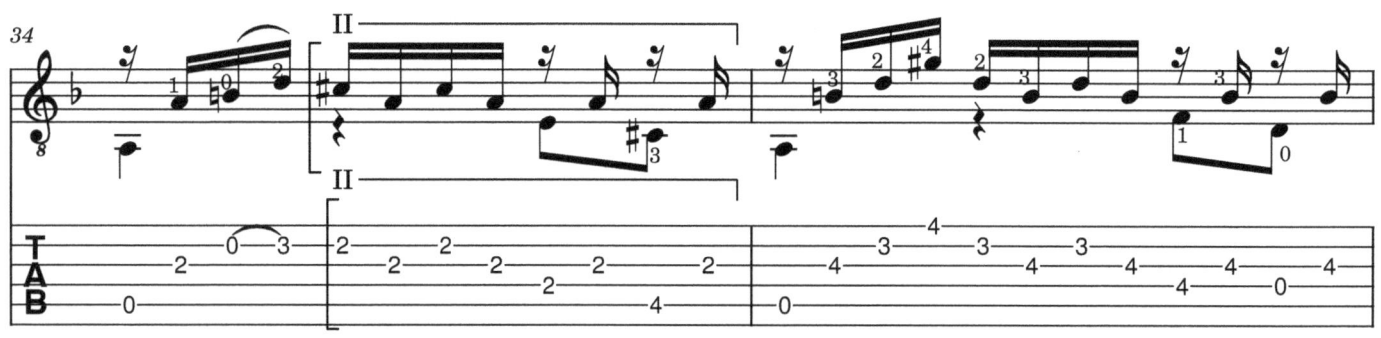
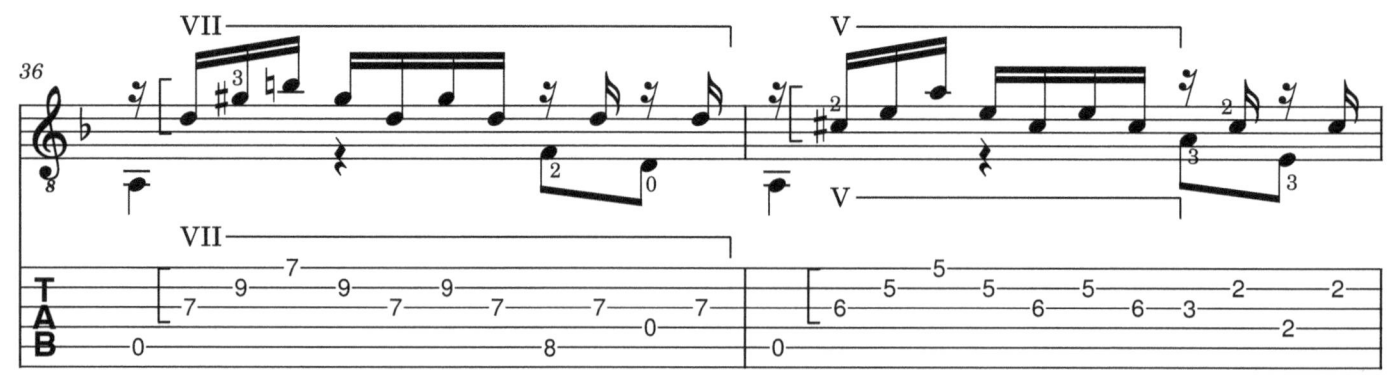

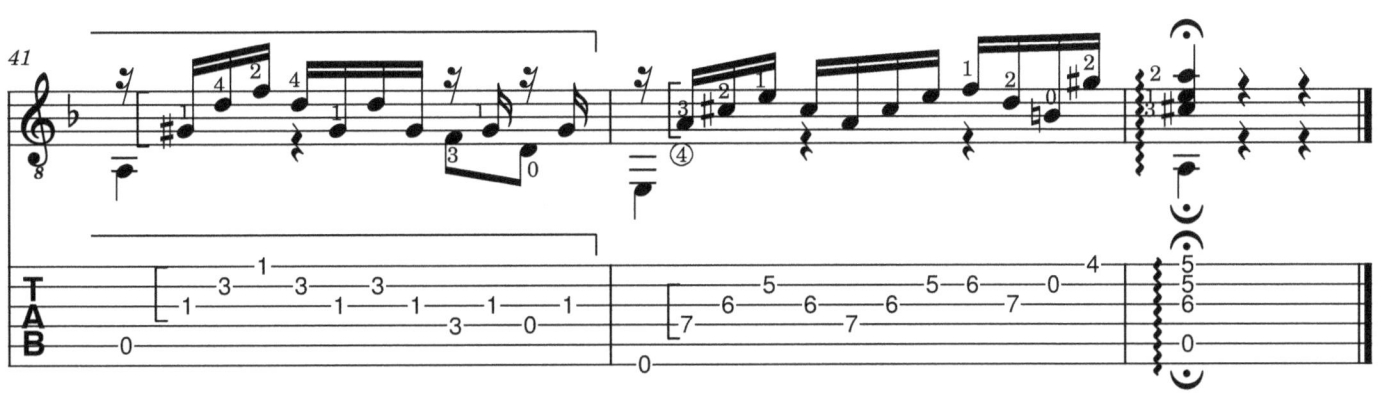

Classical Era Composers

Fernando Sor (1778-1839)

Fernando Sor was a Spanish classical guitarist and composer. He is best known for his guitar compositions, but he also composed music for opera and ballet, earning acclaim for his ballet titled Cendrillon. Sor's works for guitar range from pieces for advanced players, such as Variations on a Theme of Mozart, to beginner pieces.

Mauro Giuliani (1781-1829)

Mauro Giuliani was an italian guitarist and composer, and is considered by many to be one of the leading guitarist virtuosos of the early nineteenth century. He was a prolific composer, writing over 150 pieces for the guitar, as well as many chamber compositions for the violin, voice, flute, piano, and chamber orchestra.

Dionisio Aguado (1784-1849)

Dionisio Aguado was a Spanish classical guitarist and composer. Born in Madrid, he studied with Miguel Garcia. In 1825, Aguado visited Paris, where he met and became friends with lived with Fernando Sor. Aguado's major work Escuela de Guitarra was a guitar tutorial published in 1825. Dionisio Aguado has attained lasting fame through his method for guitar, which is still in print today.

Andantino
Opus 50 No.27

Mauro Giuliani (1781-1829)

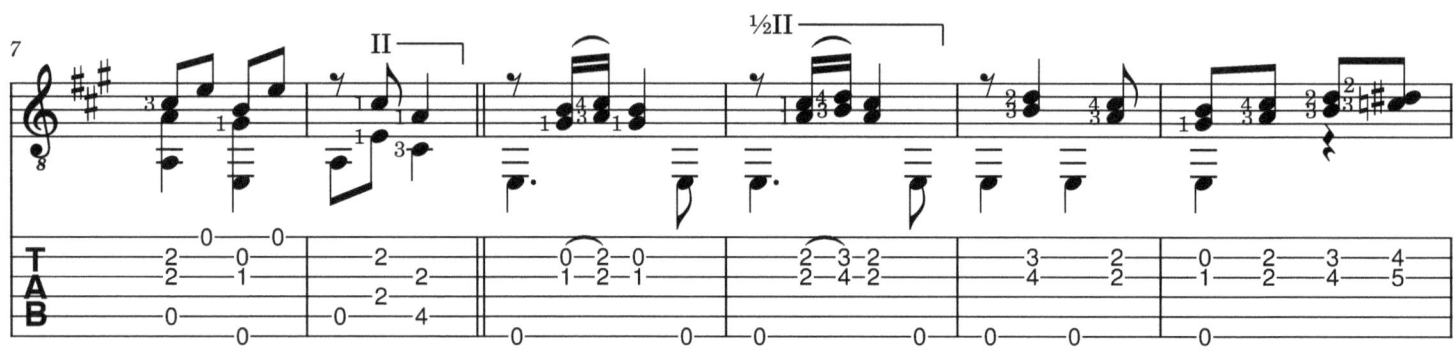
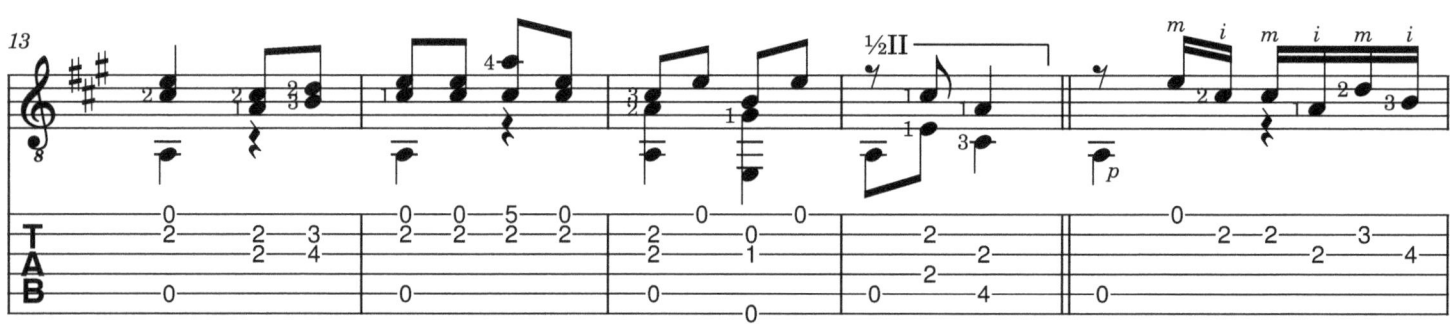
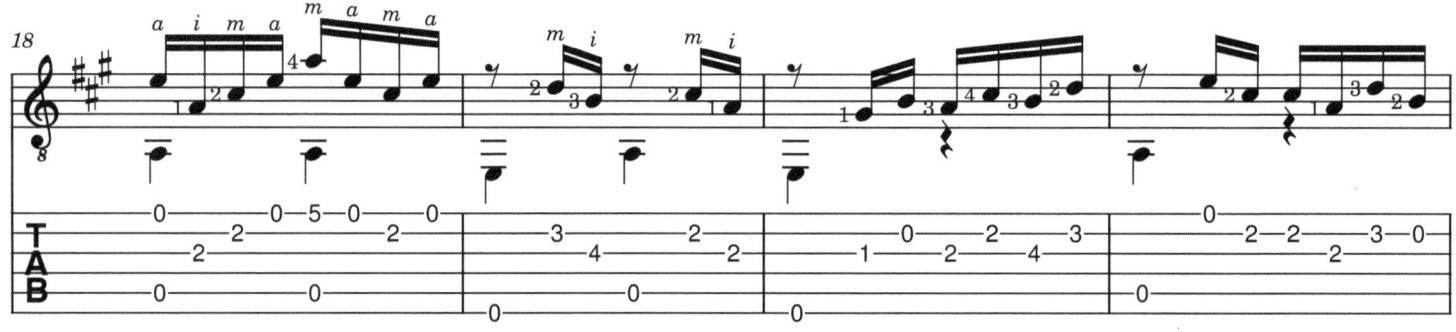
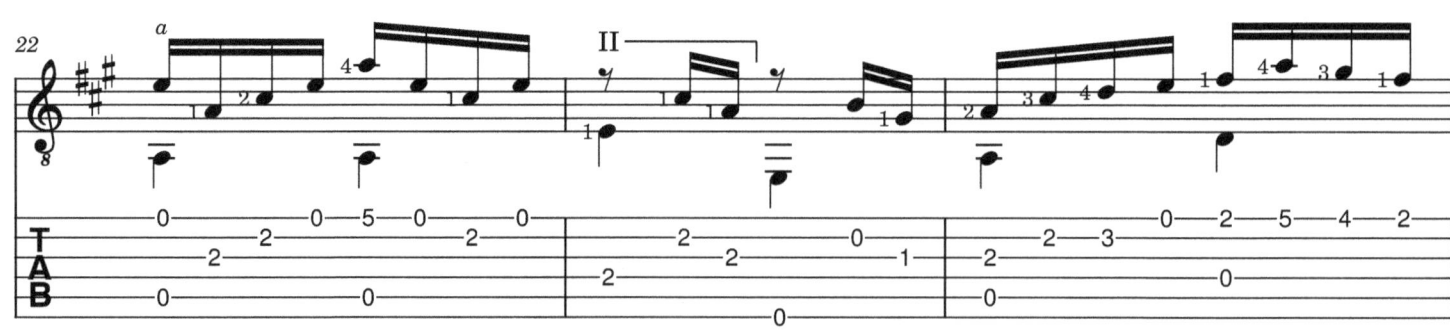

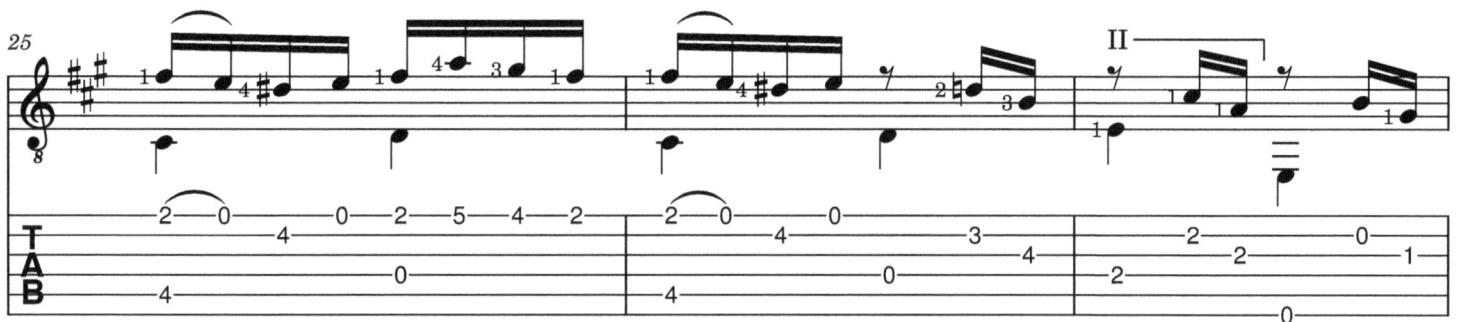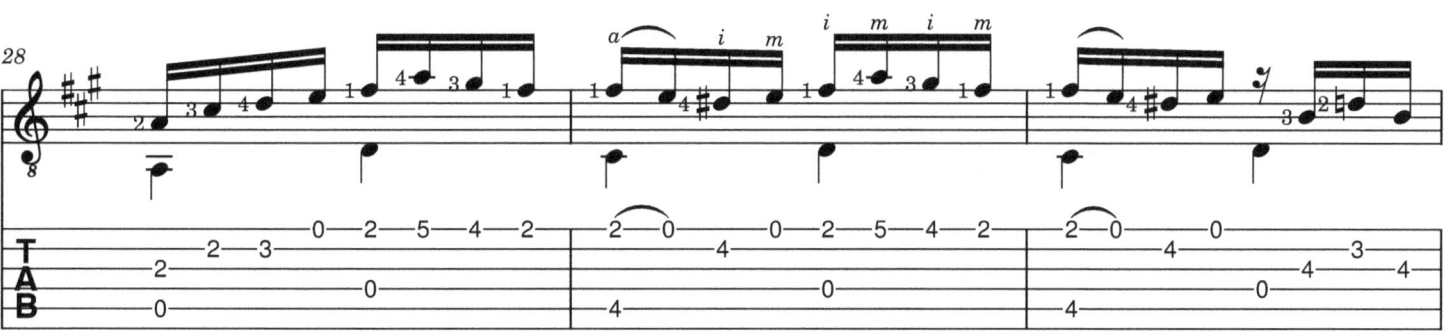

Andantino
Opus 50 No.28

Mauro Giuliani (1781-1829)

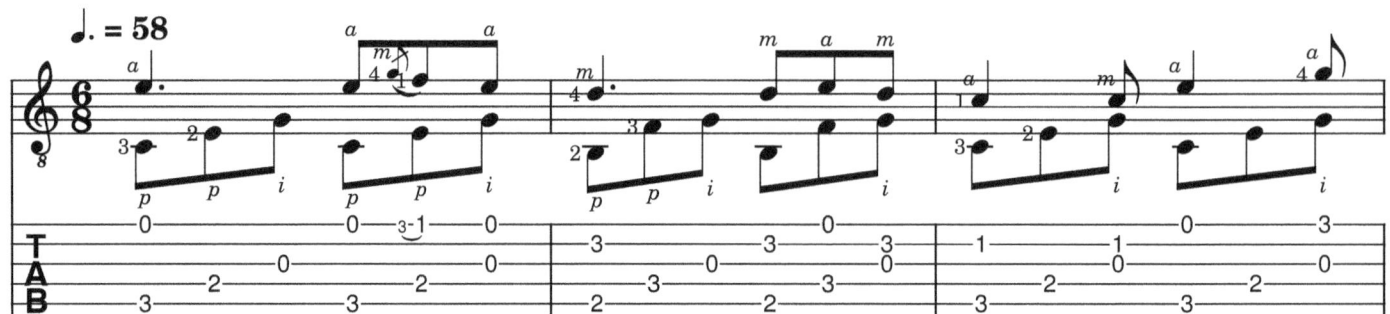
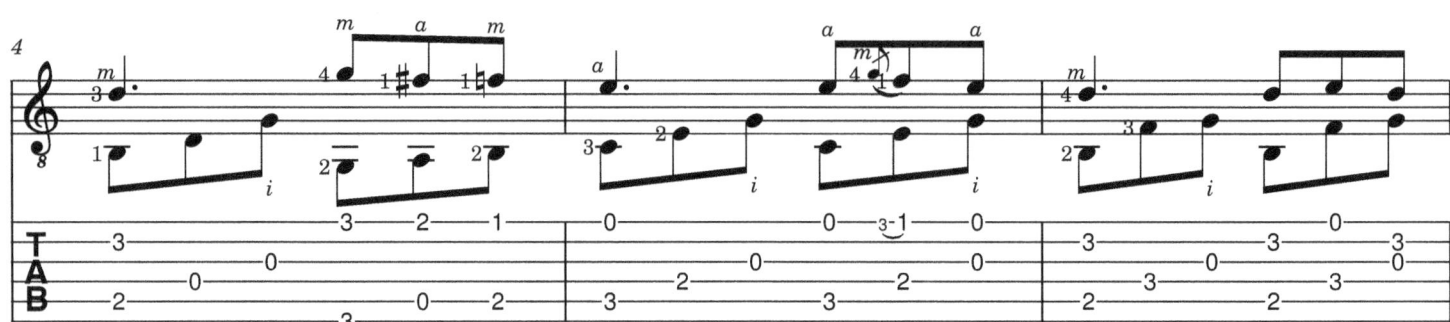

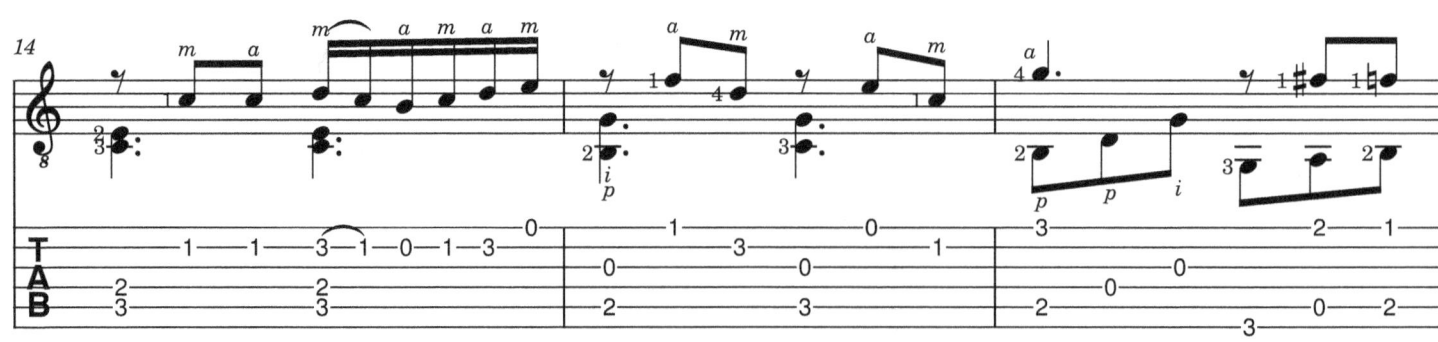

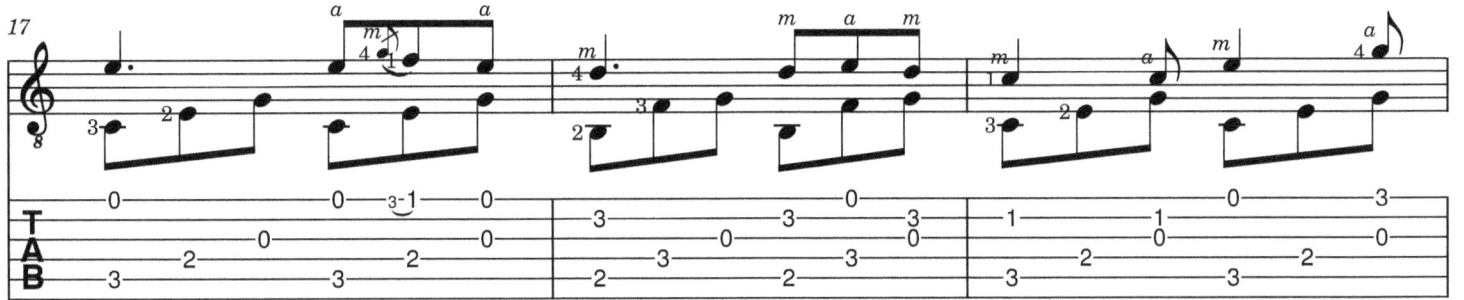
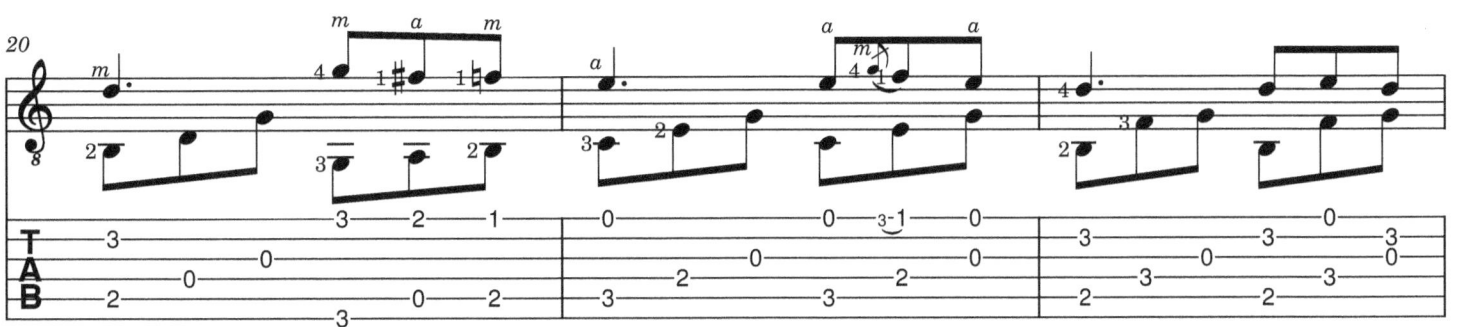
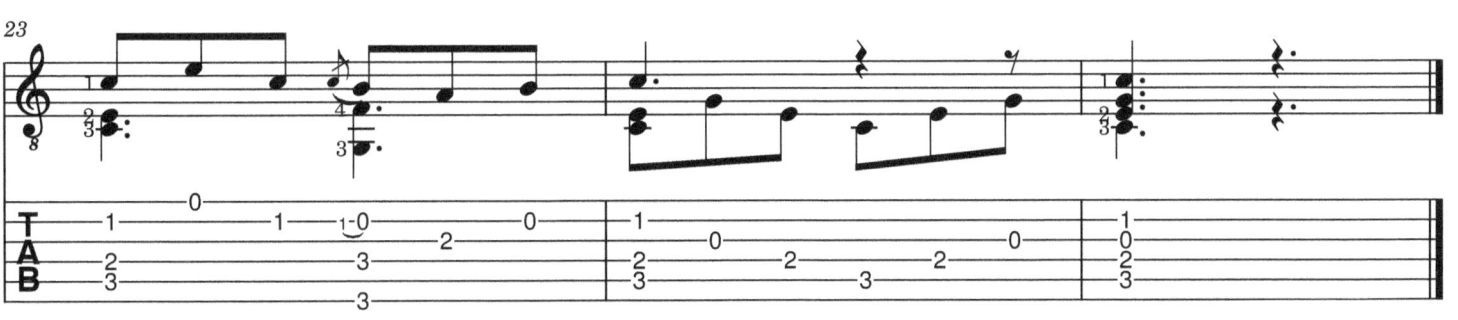

Andante

Fernando Sor (1778 - 1839)

Etude n°17 op.35

Fernando Sor (1778 - 1839)

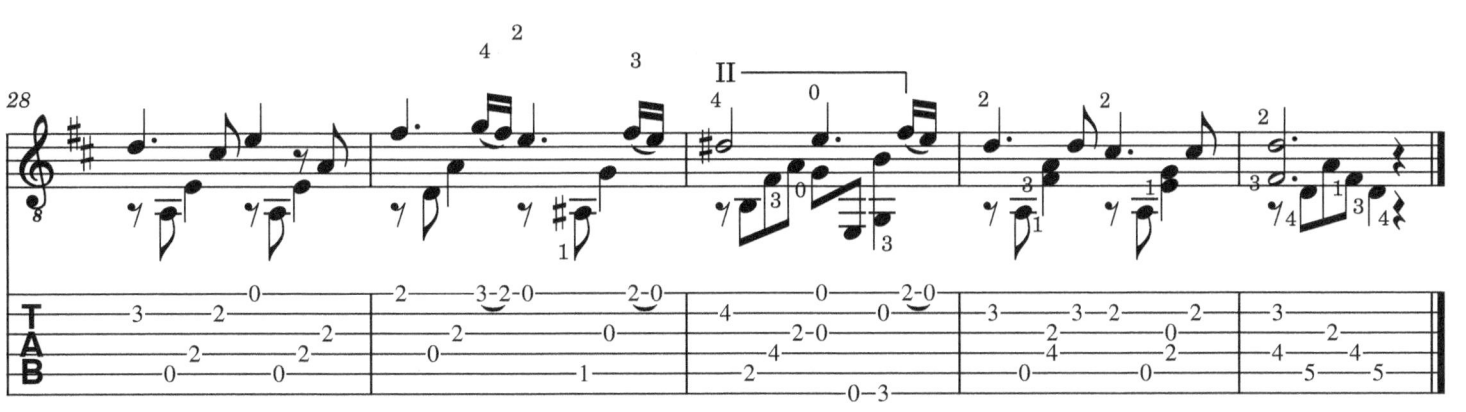

Etude No.22 Op.35

Fernando Sor (1778 - 1839)

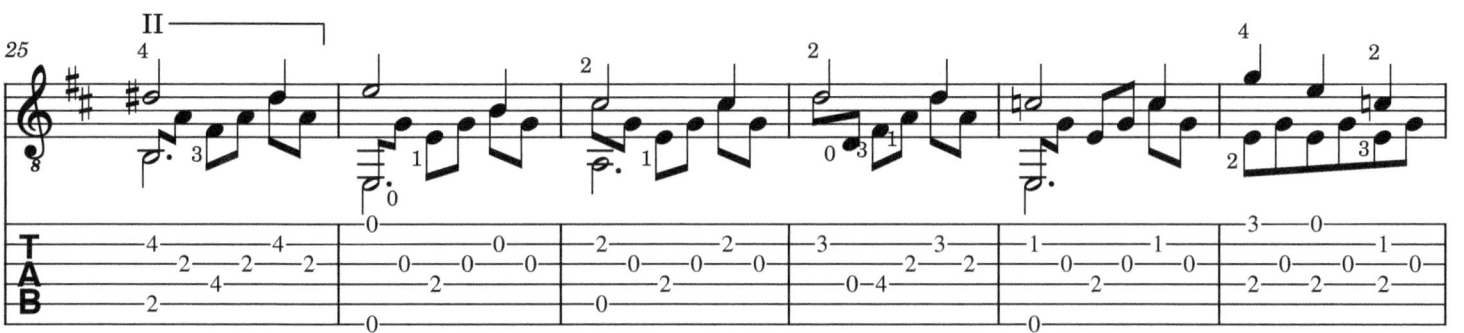

Allegretto

Dionisio Aguado (1784-1849)

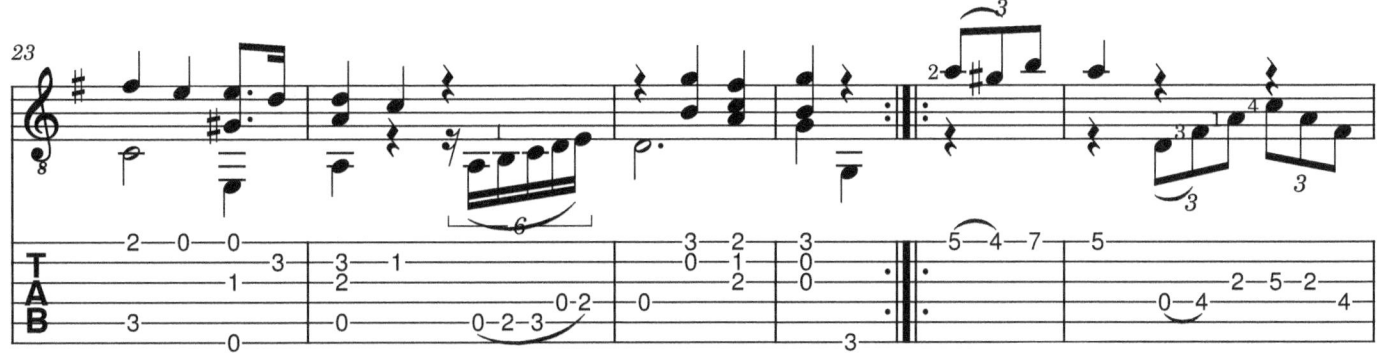
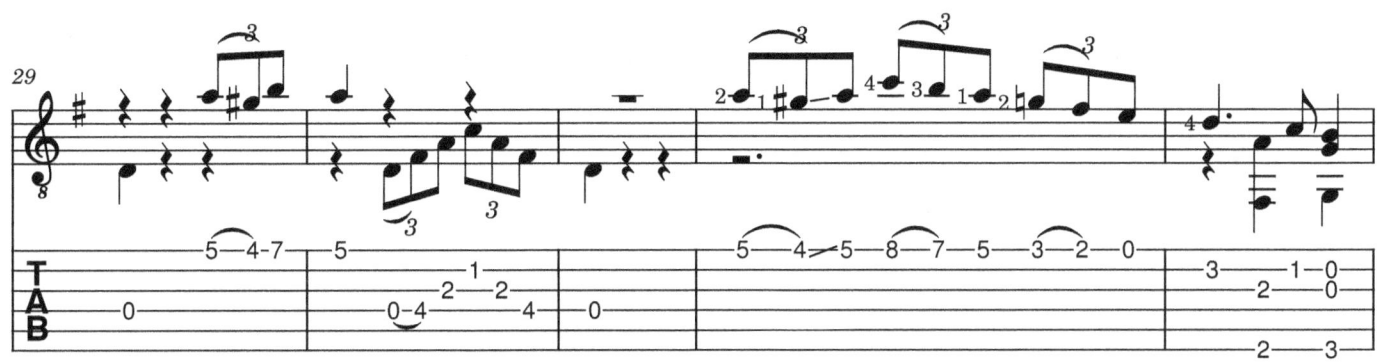

Waltz

Dionisio Aguado (1784-1849)

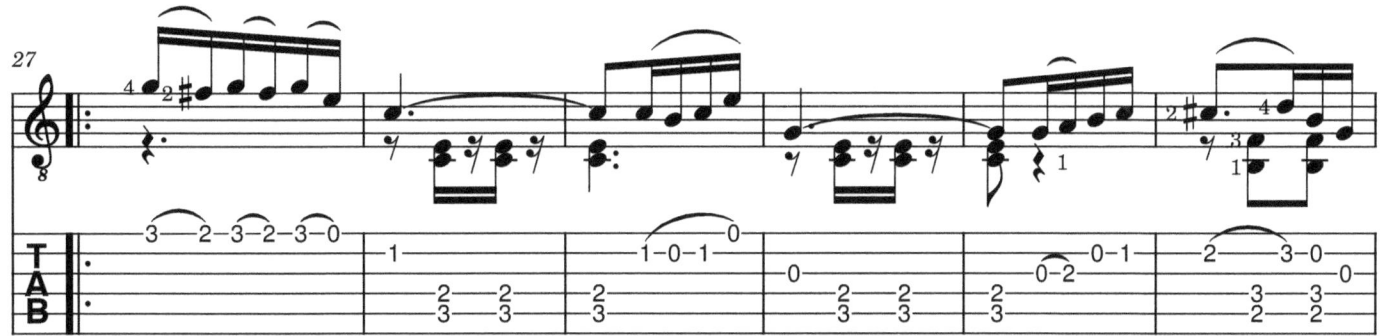
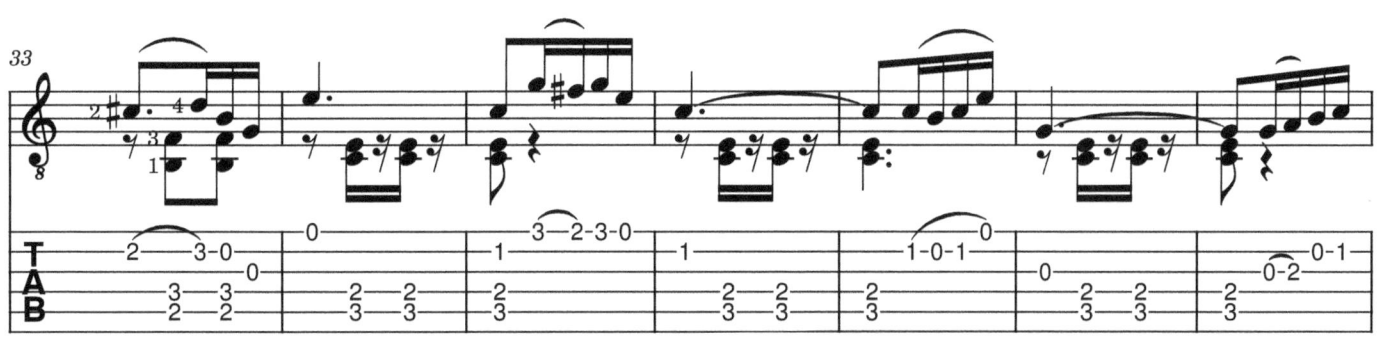

Waltz

Fernando Sor (1778-1839)

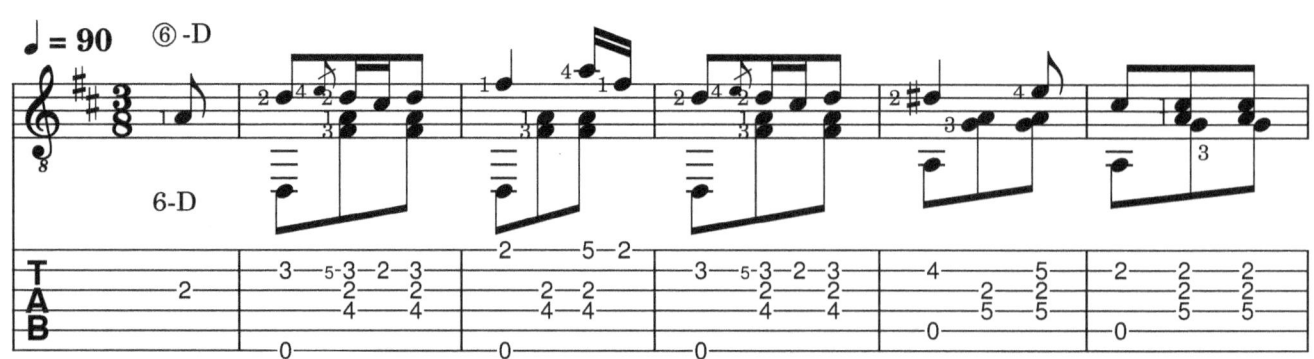

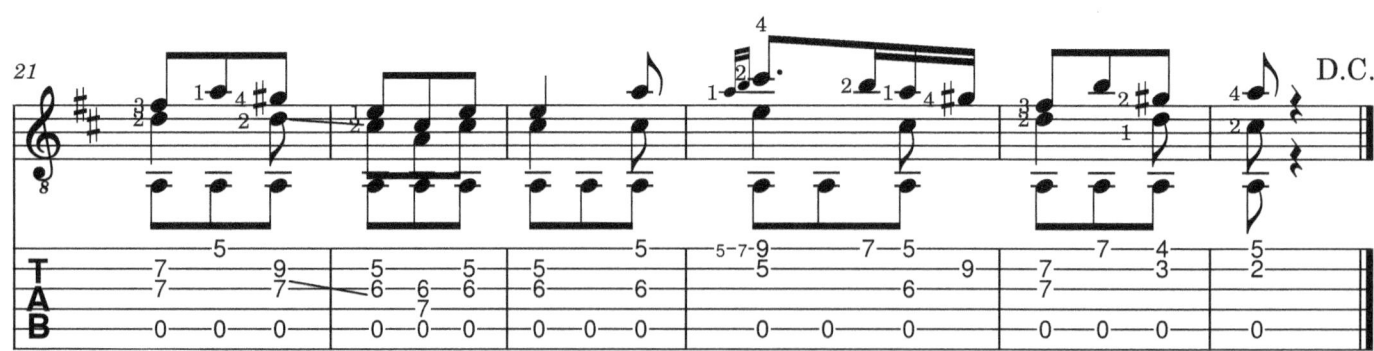

Menuet

Fernando Sor (1778 - 1839)

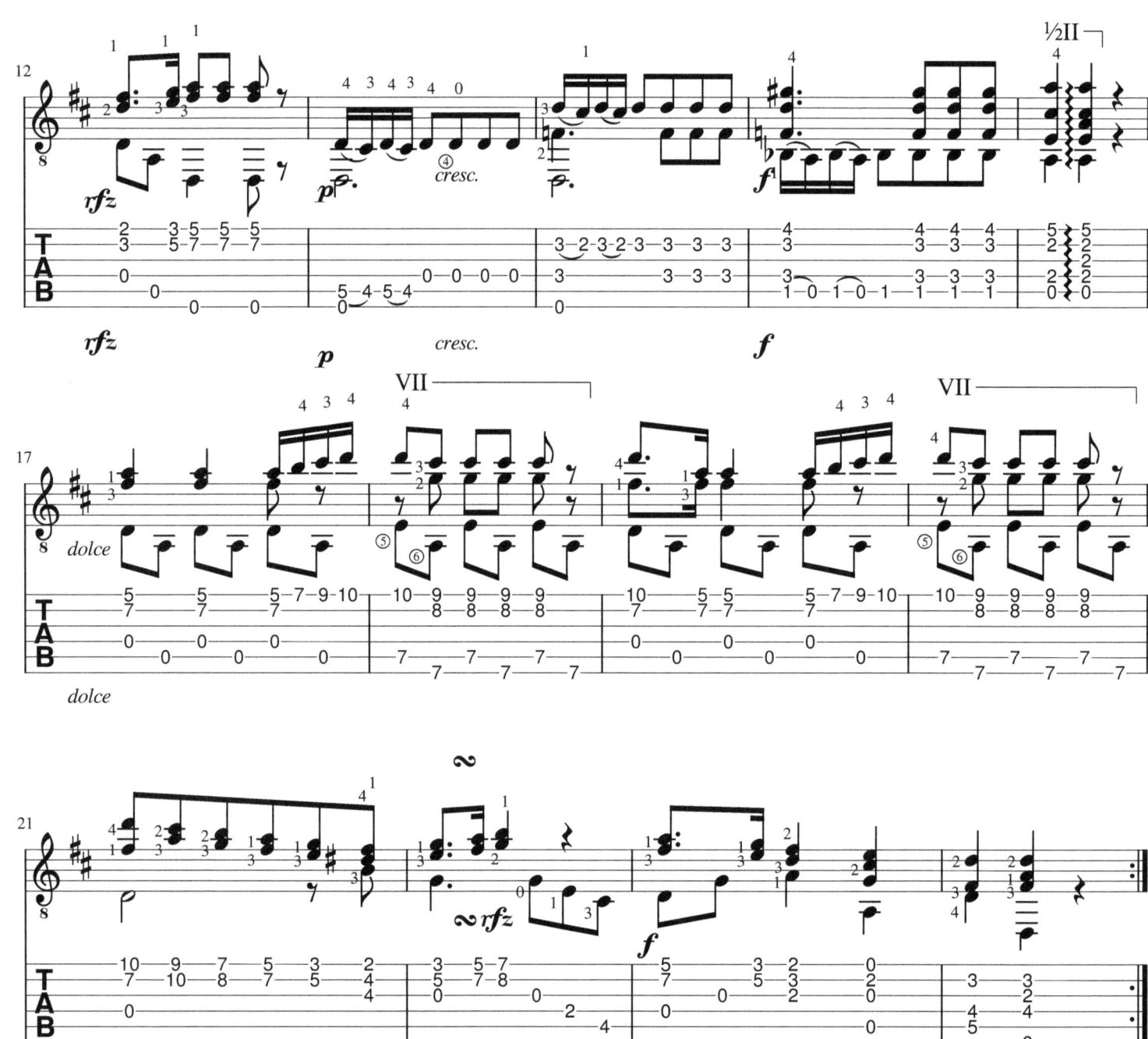

Romantic Era Composers

Matteo Carcassi (1792-1853)

Matteo Carcassi was a famous Italian guitarist and composer. Carcassi began with the piano, but learned guitar when still a child. He quickly gained a reputation as a virtuoso concert guitarist. Carcassi wrote a method for guitar (op. 59) that remains valuable, relevant and interesting, blending technical skills and brilliant romantic music.

Johann Kaspar Mertz (1806-1856)

János Gáspár Mertz was born in Pozsony, Kingdom of Hungary, now Bratislava (Slovakia). A virtuoso, he established a solid reputation as a performer. Mertz's guitar music, followed the pianistic models of Chopin, Mendelssohn, Schubert and Schumann, rather than the classical models of Mozart and Haydn (as did Sor and Aguado), or the bel canto style of Rossini (as did Giuliani).

Napoleon Coste (1805 – 1883)

Napoleon is french and is a major figure in guitar composition of the mid-nineteenth century. Napoleon was taught by his mother at a very early age. Napoleon later became Fernando Sor's student and quickly established himself as the leading French virtuoso guitarist. Napoleon is the first composer to transcribe guitar music of the 17th century to the modern era.

Francisco Tarrega (1852-1909)

Tárrega is considered to have laid the foundations for 20th century classical guitar and for increasing interest in the guitar as a recital instrument. Tárrega preferred small intimate performances over the concert stage. Some believe this was because he played without the nails needed for volume. Others say this was related to his childhood trauma.

José Ferrer (1835-1916)

José Ferrer was a Spanish guitarist and composer, born in Spain. Ferrer studied guitar with his father, a guitarist and collector of sheet music, before continuing his studies with José Brocá. In 1882, he left Spain for Paris in order to teach at the Institut Rudy and at the Académie Internationale de Musique.

Barcarolle

Napoleon Coste (1805 - 1883)

Etude No.13

Napoleon Coste (1806 - 1883)

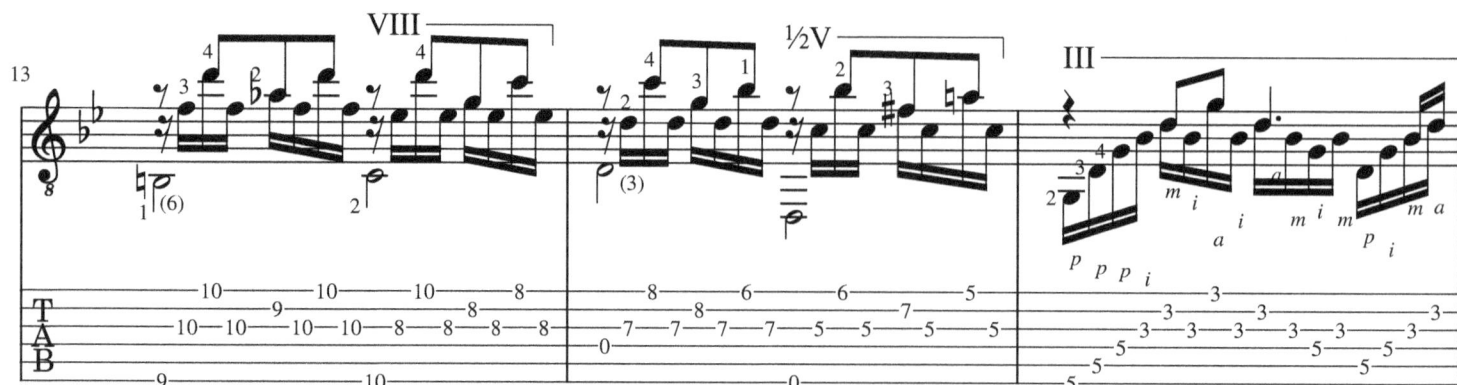

Waltz

Napoleon Coste (1805 - 1883)

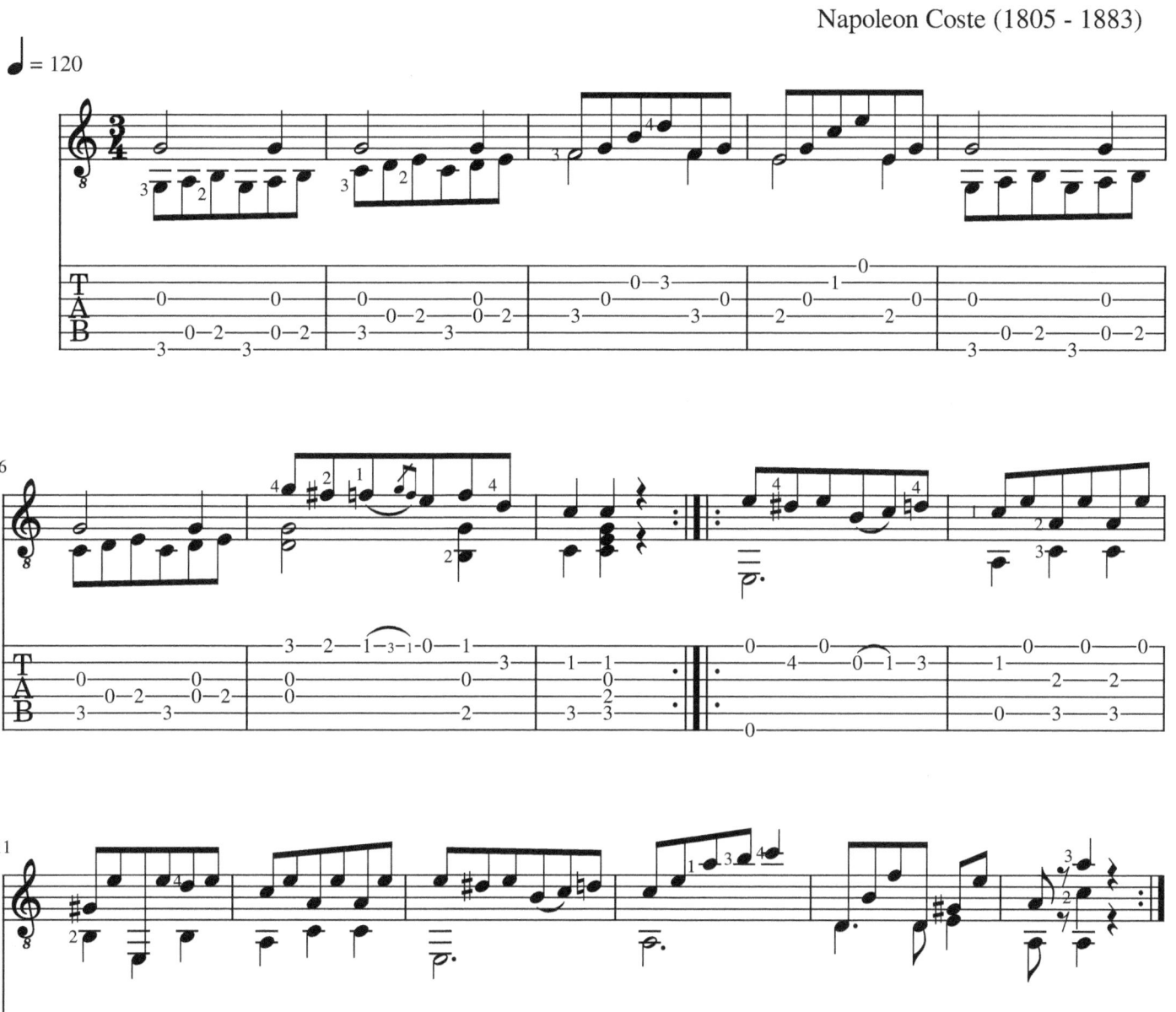

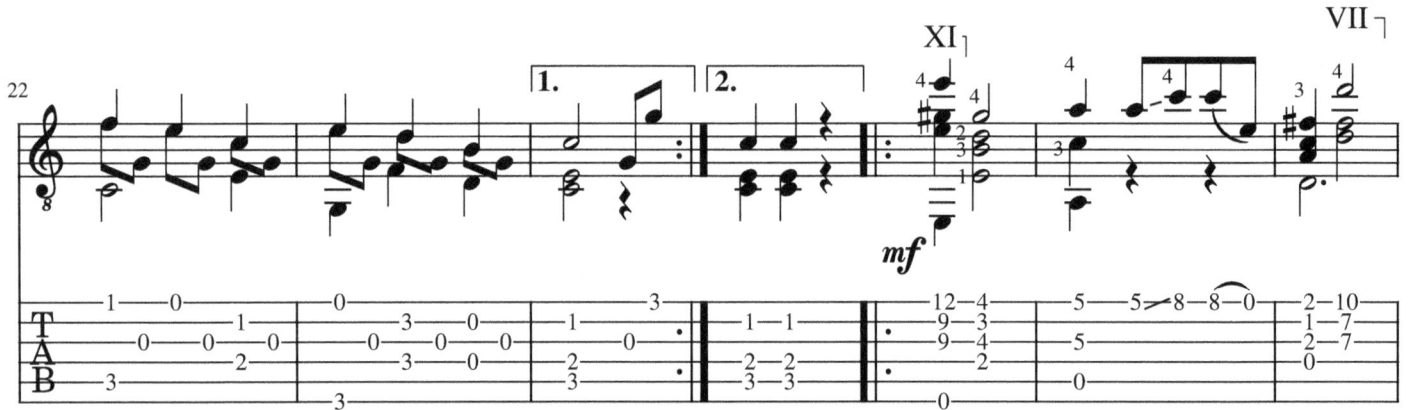
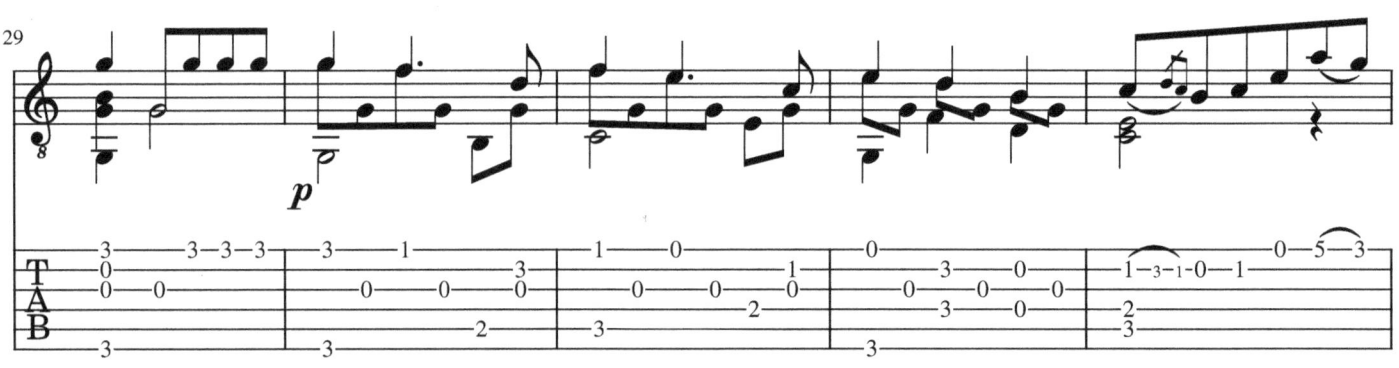
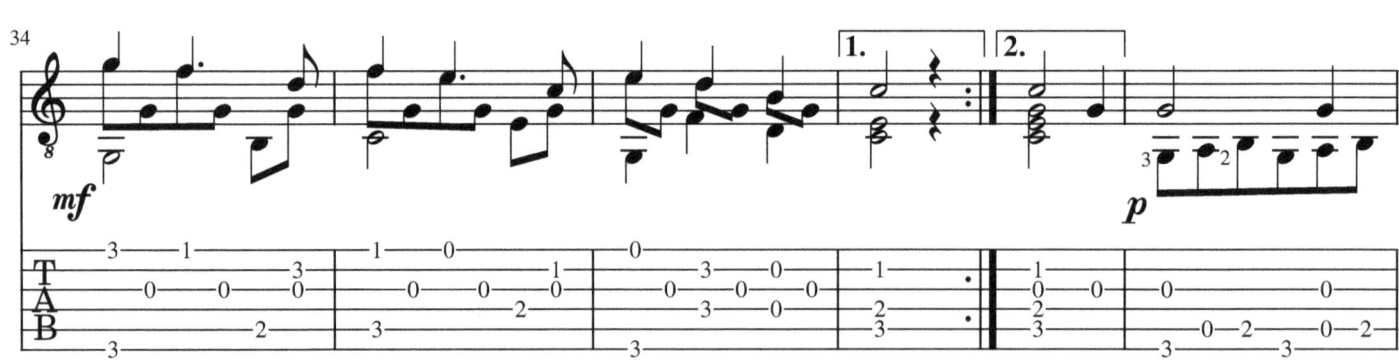

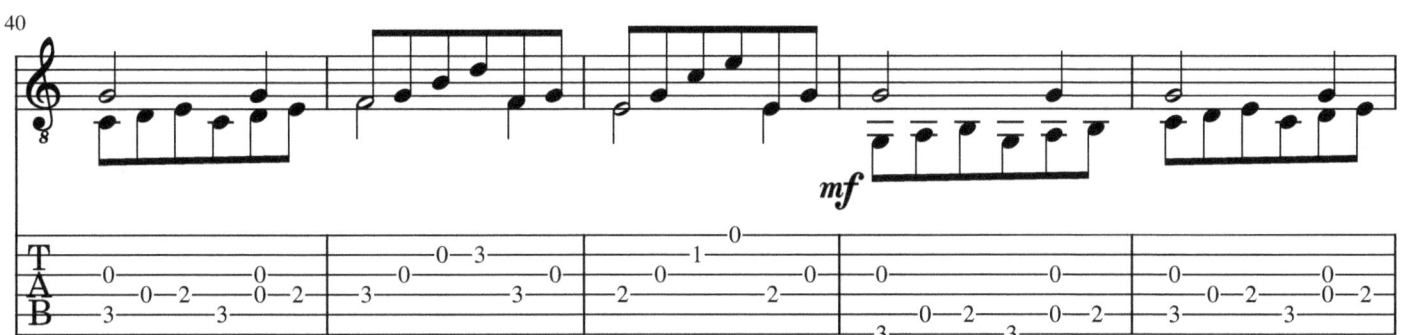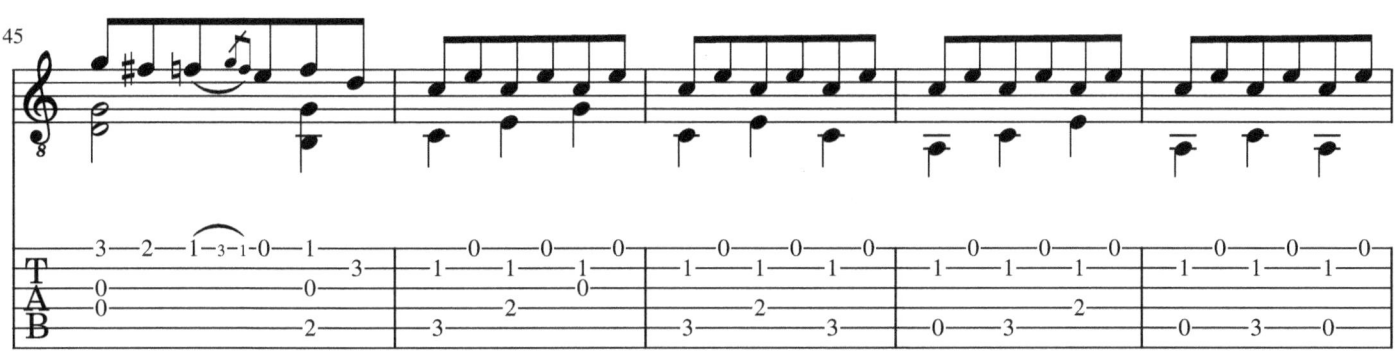

Etude No.1

Francisco Tarrega (1852-1909)

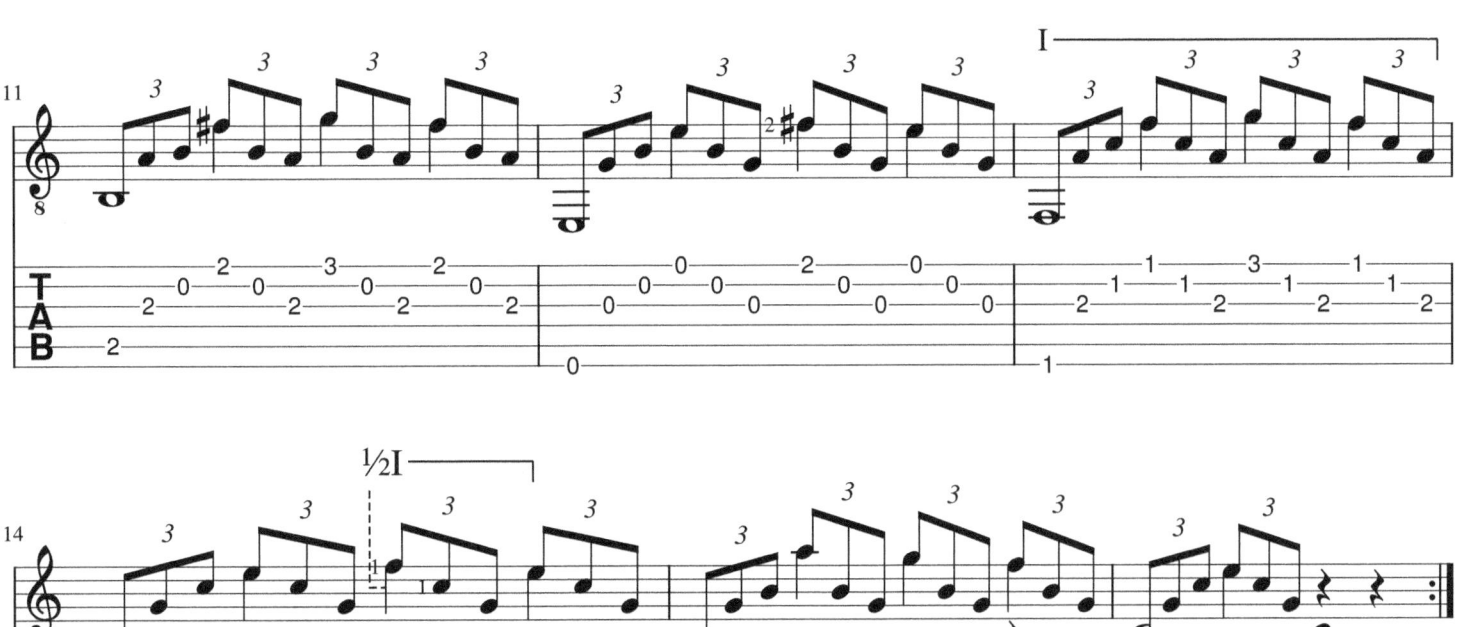

Adelita
Mazurka

Francisco Tarrega (1852-19[0?])

Etude No.3 Op.60

Matteo Carcassi (1796-1853)

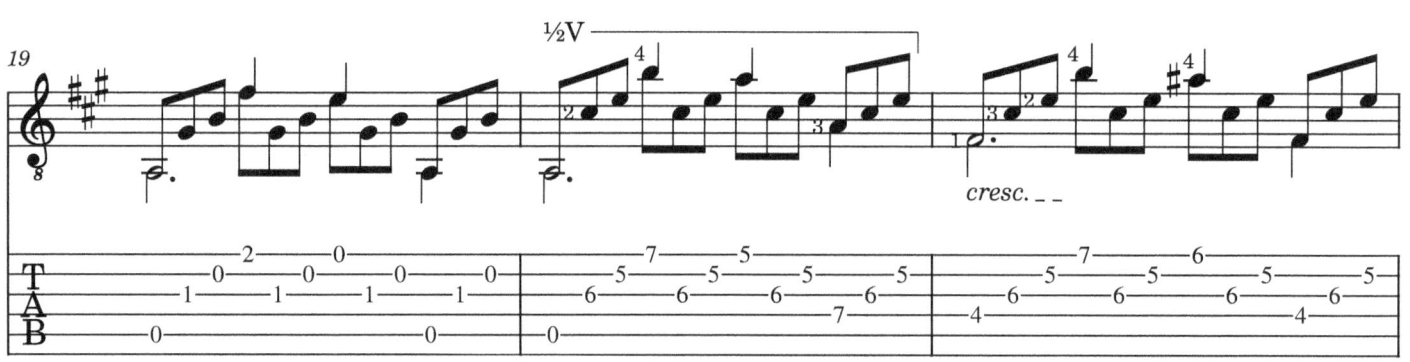
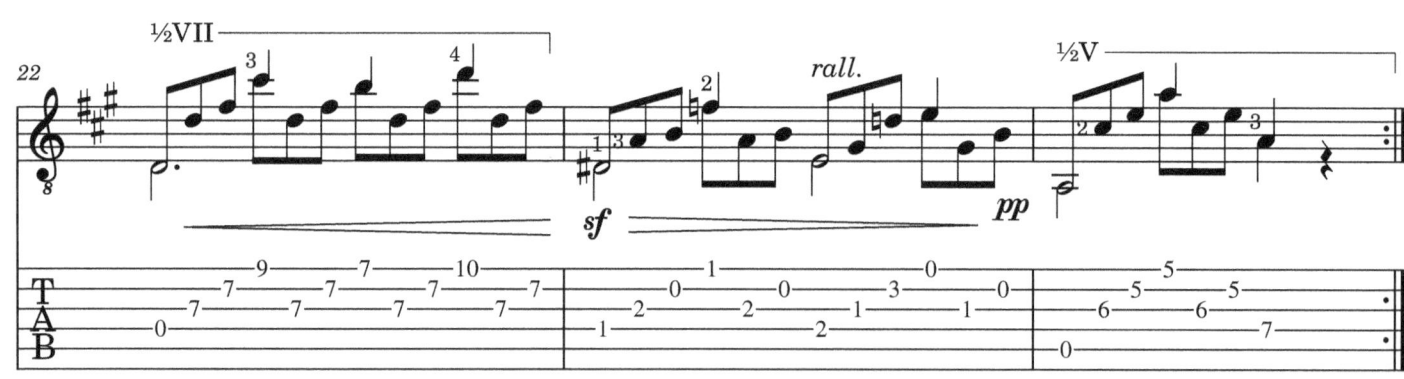

Etude No.16 Op.60

Matteo Carcassi (1792 -1853)

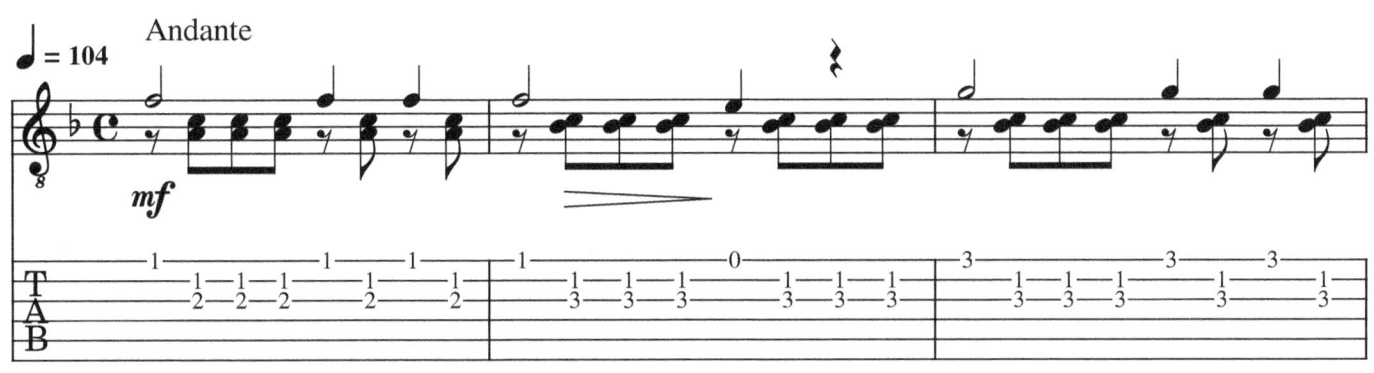

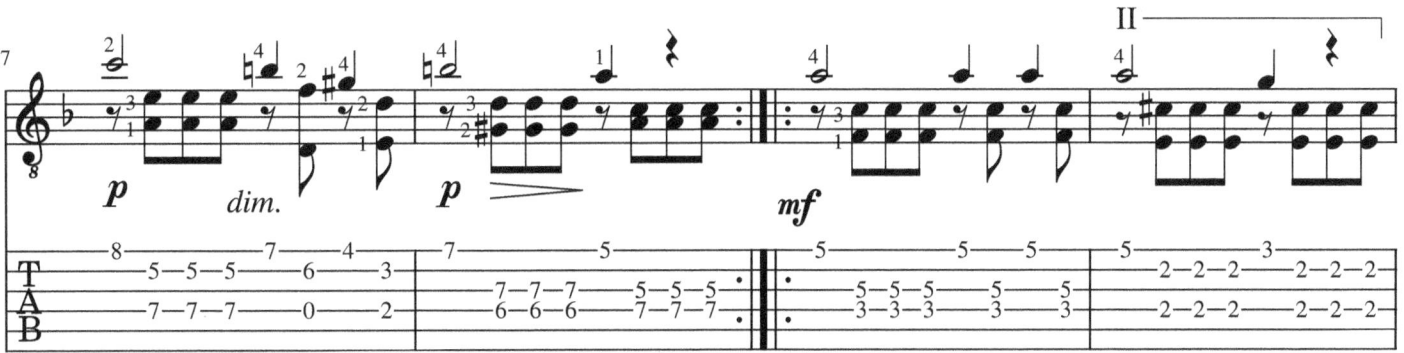

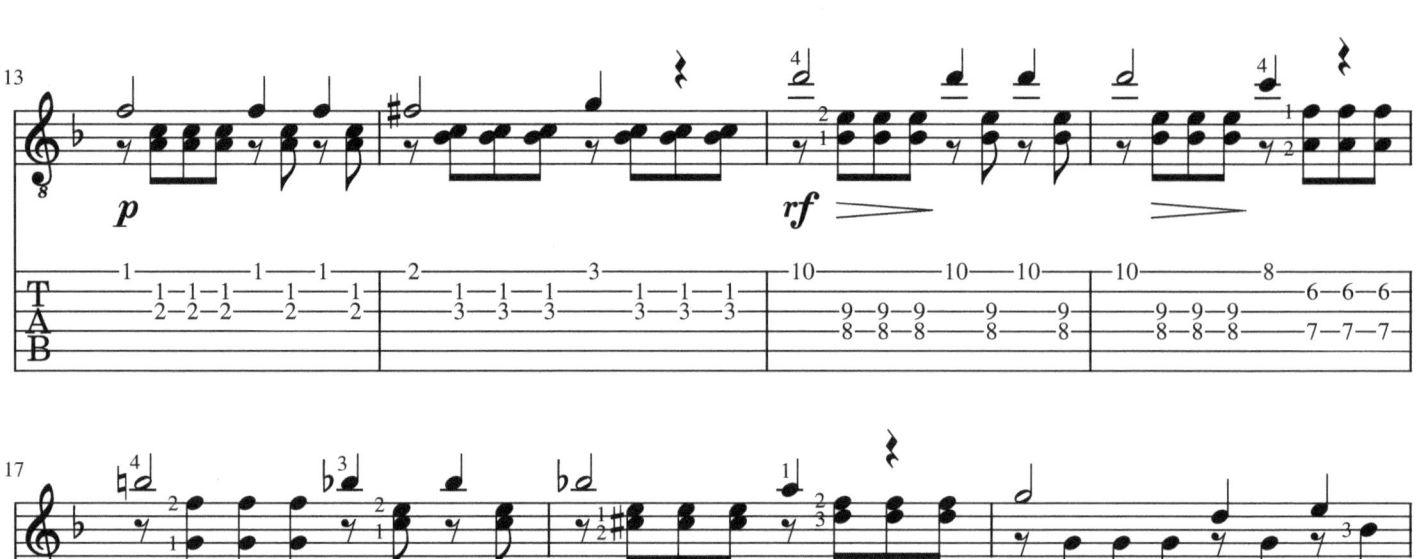

Nocturne
Opus 4 No.2 Part1

Johann Kaspar Mertz (1806 - 1856)

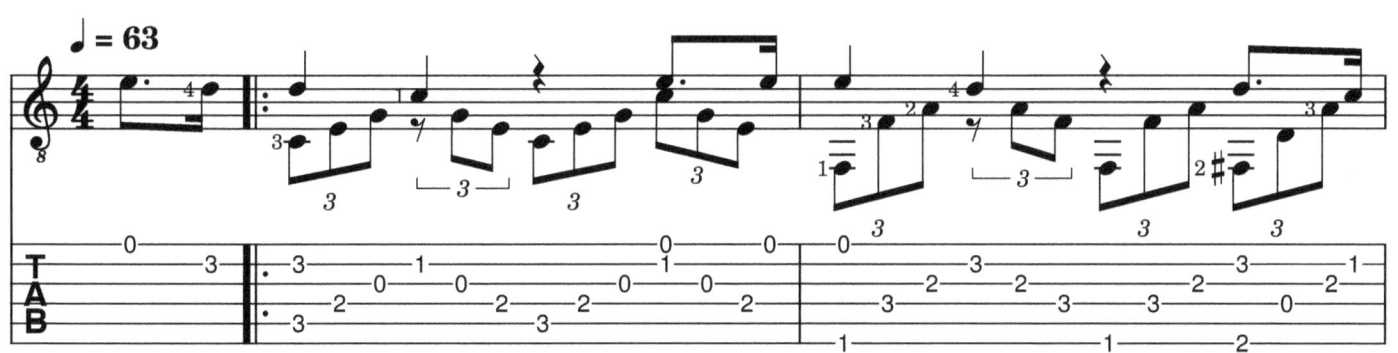

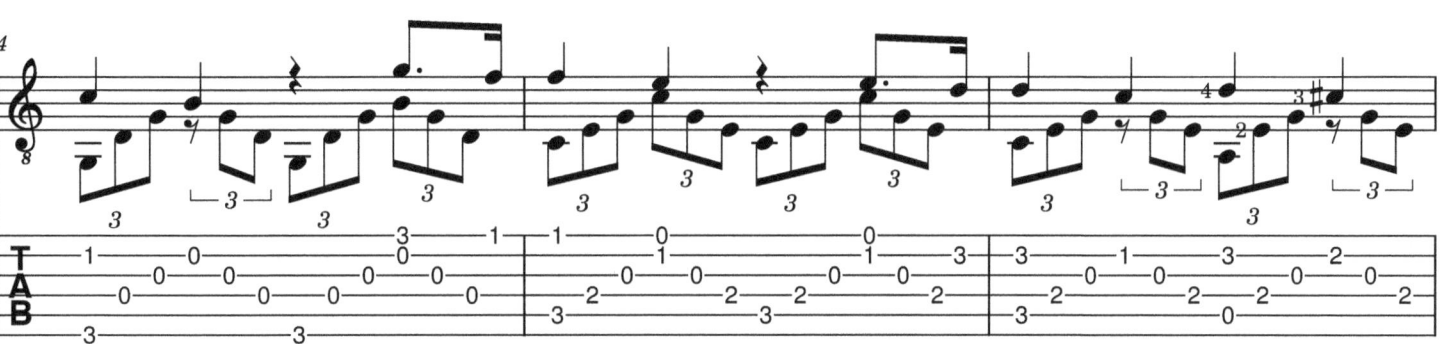

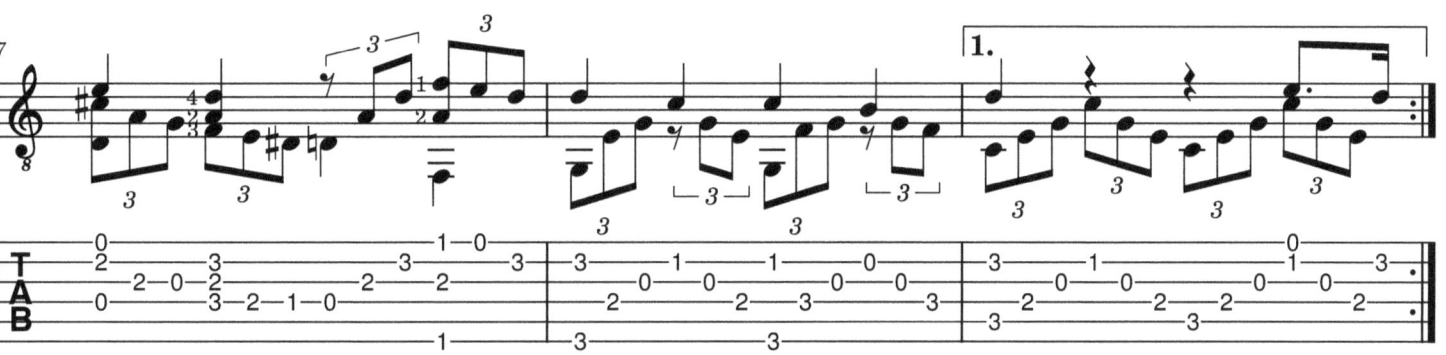

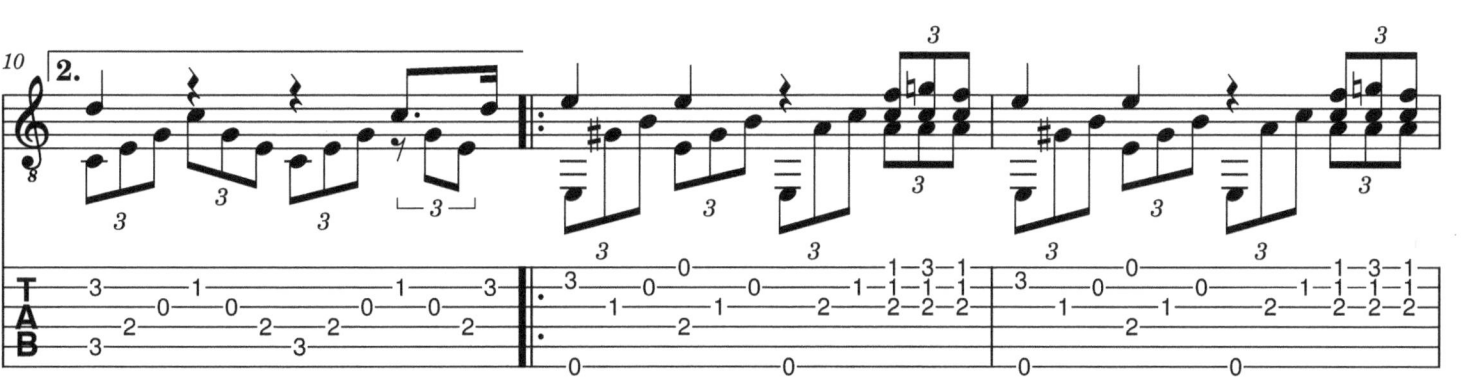

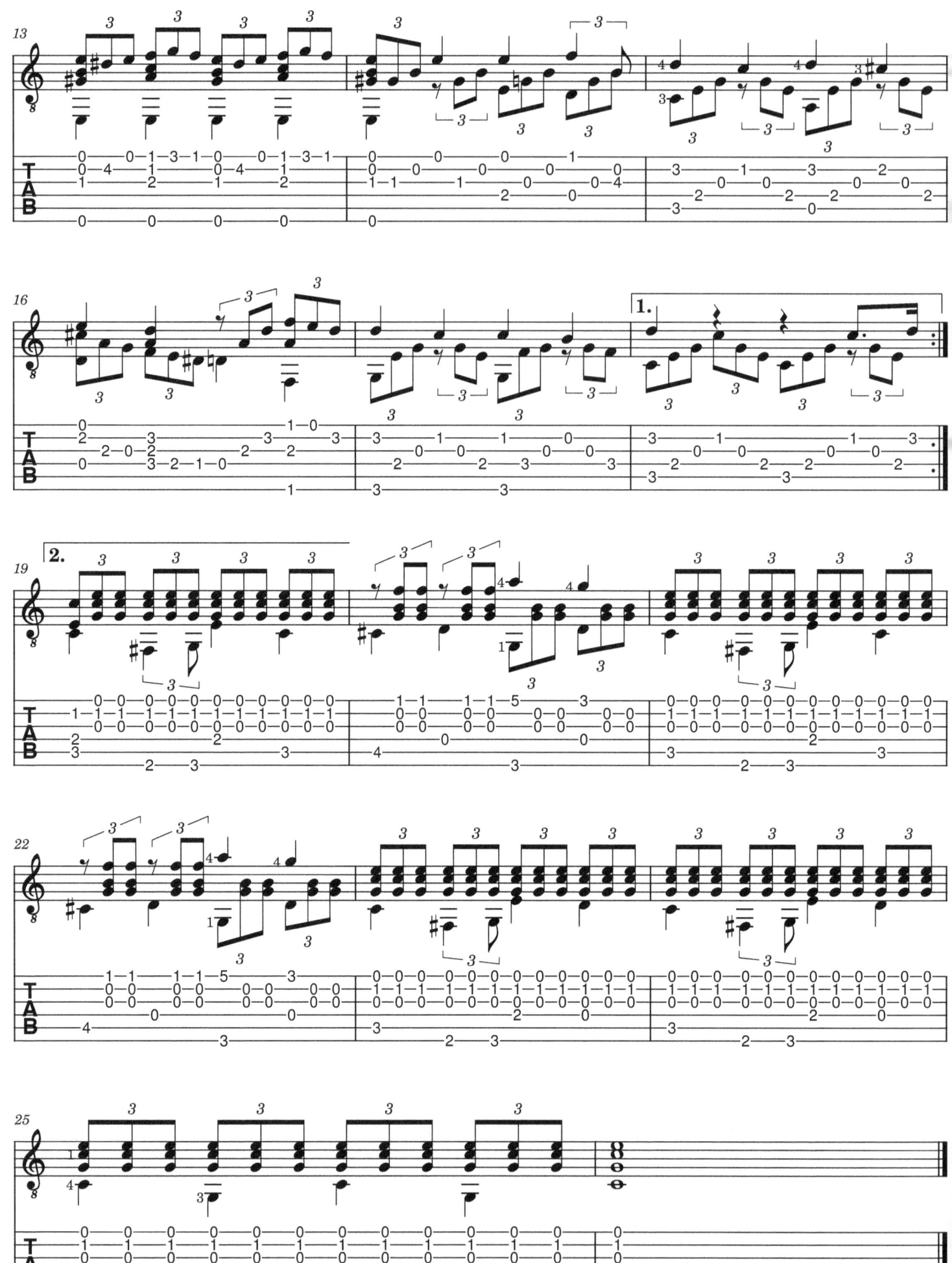

Ejercicio

Jose Ferrer (1835 - 1916)

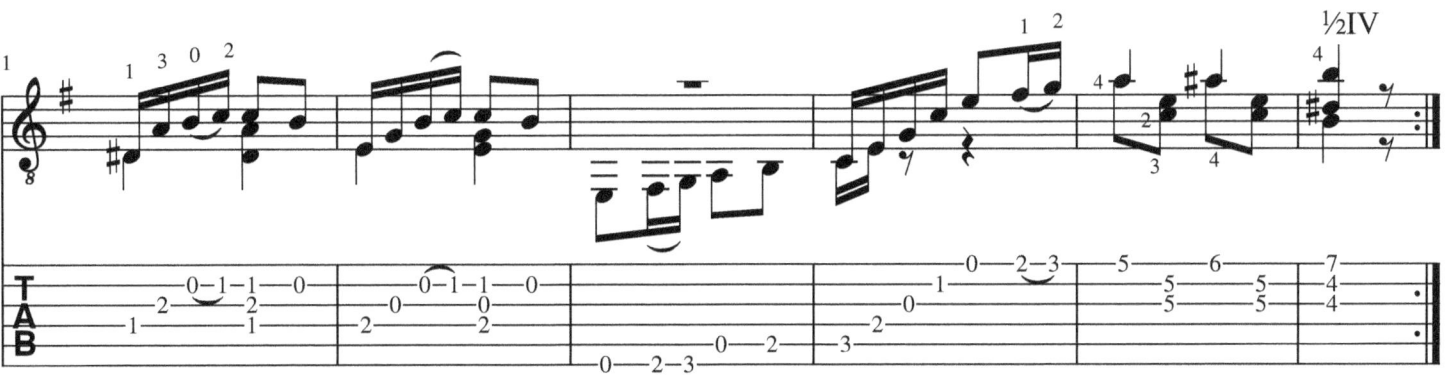
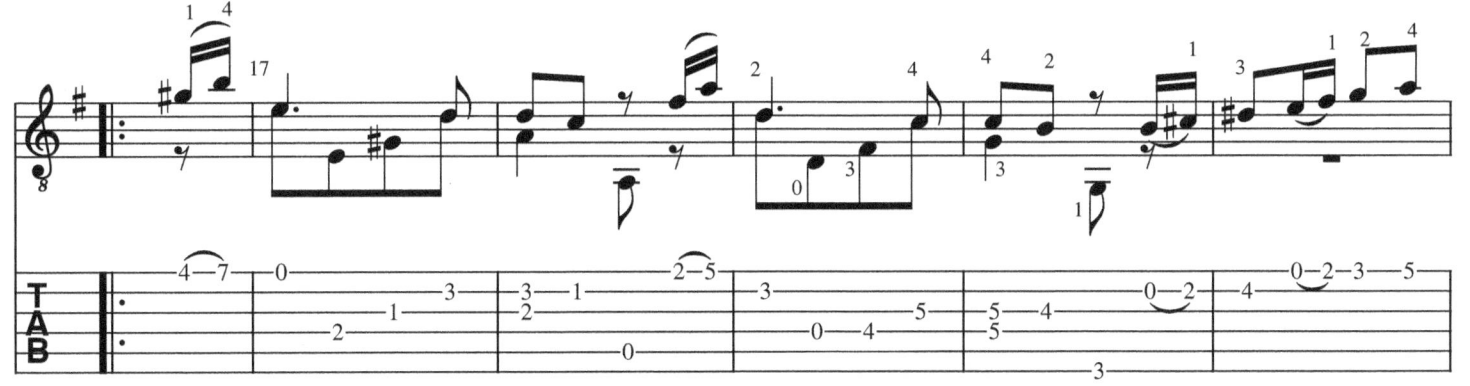

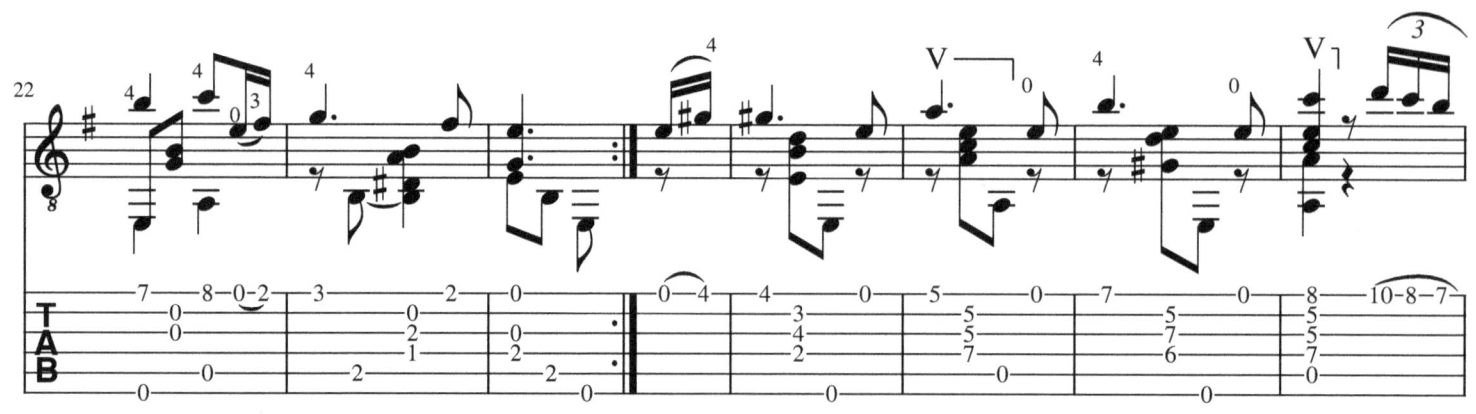

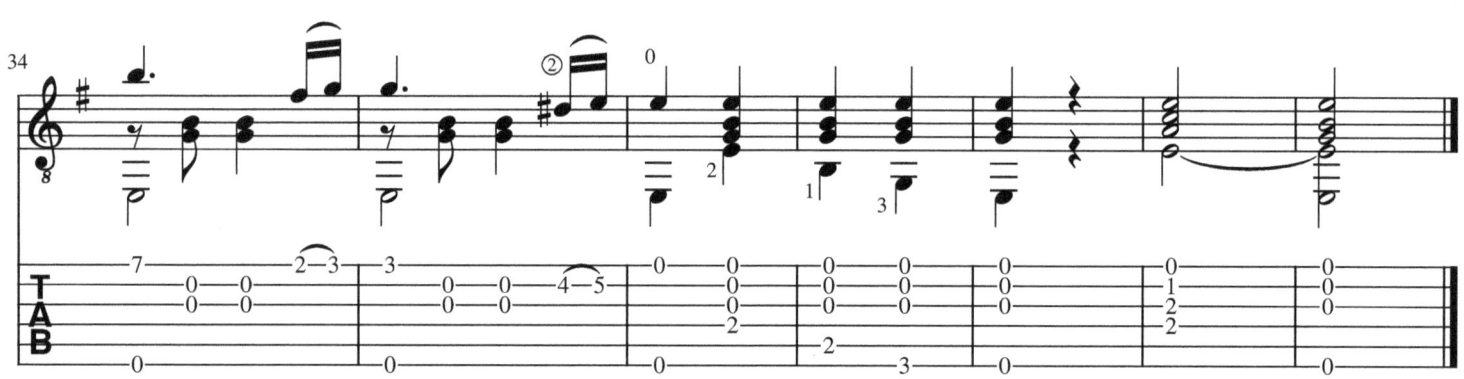

Tango n°3 op.50

Jose Ferrer (1835 - 1916)

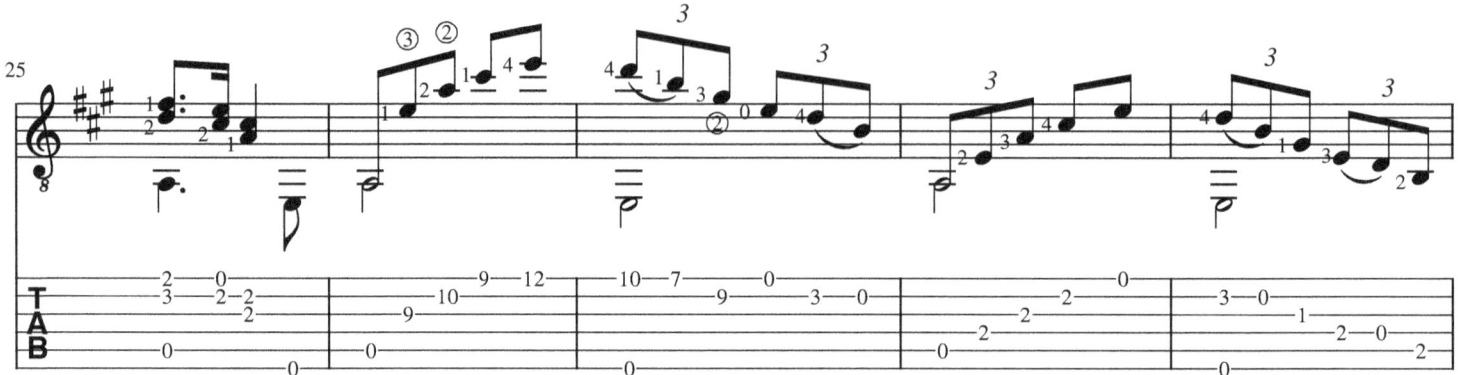
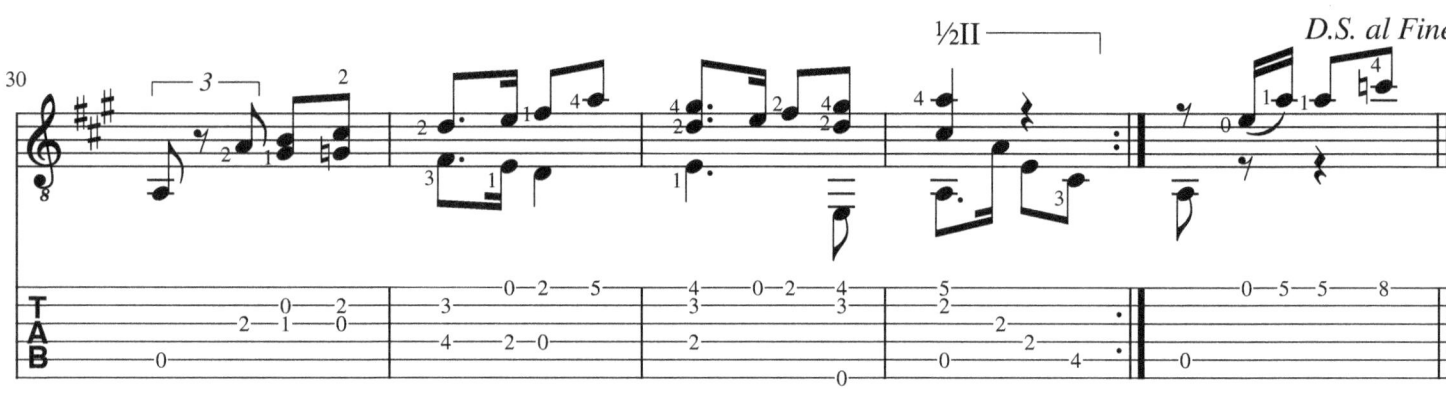

Multicultural/Traditional

Domingos Semenzato (1908-1993)

Domingos Semenzato, Brazilian composer and guitarist (1908-1993), began his musical activity as a member of chôros groups playing the guitar and the cavaquinho (a small stringed instrument similar to the Canarian timple). Later, he perfected his classical guitar studies in Sao Paulo, becoming a great soloist.

João Pernambuco (1883-1947)

João Teixeira Guimarães (1883-1947), better known as João Pernambuco, is one of the founders of the Brasilian guitar choro style, and his compositions for solo violão are deservedly considered belonging to the core of classic choro, popular with guitarists, loved and admired by audiences in Brazil and elsewhere.

Greensleeves

16th century English Traditional

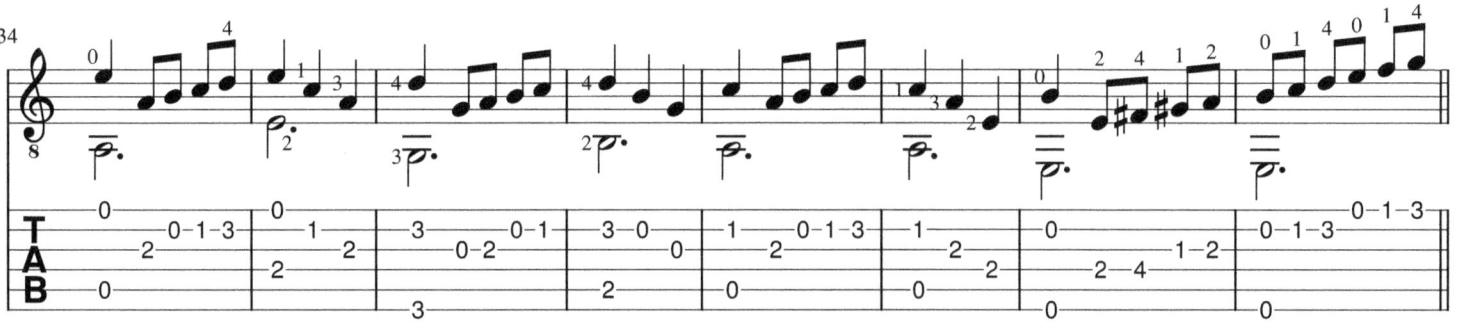
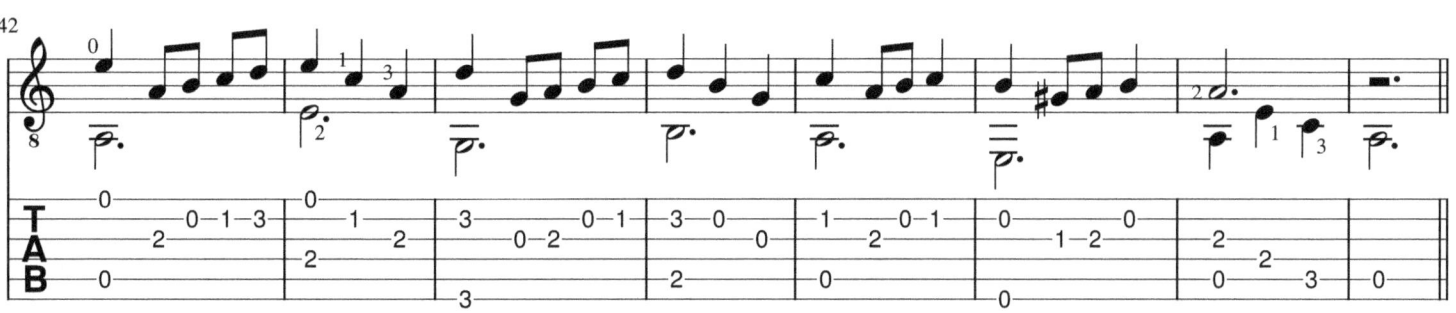
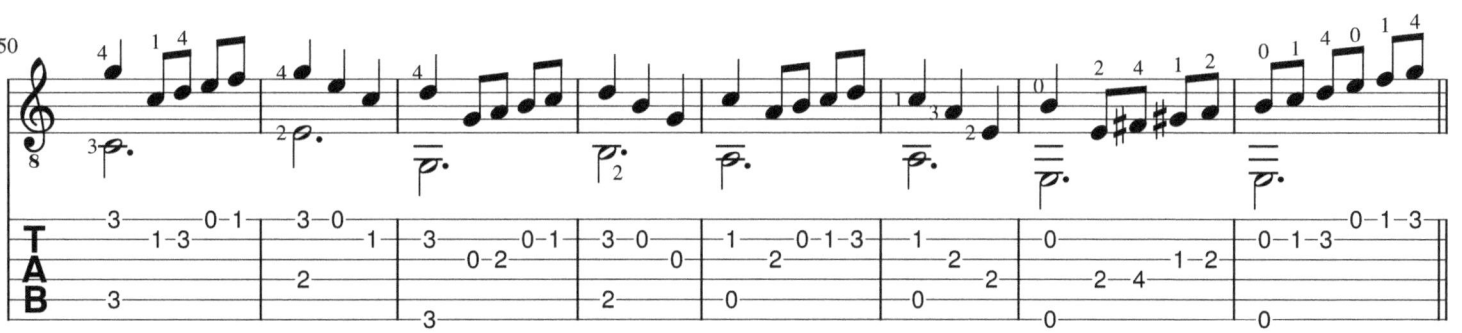

D.C. al Fine

Choro

Domingos Semenzato (1908-1993)

1.
2.
V
Hr.7
Fine
Hr.
I
D.S. al Fine

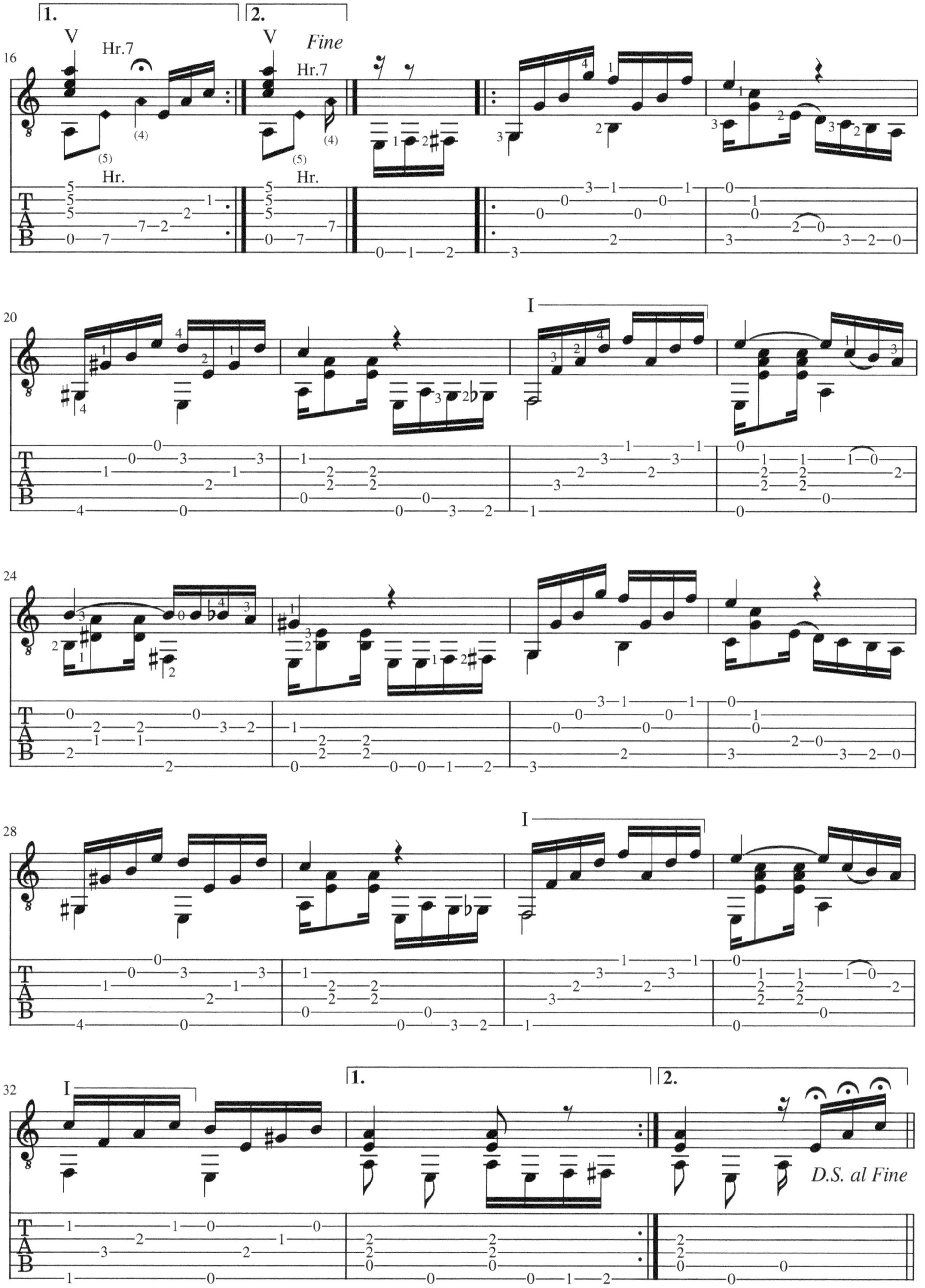

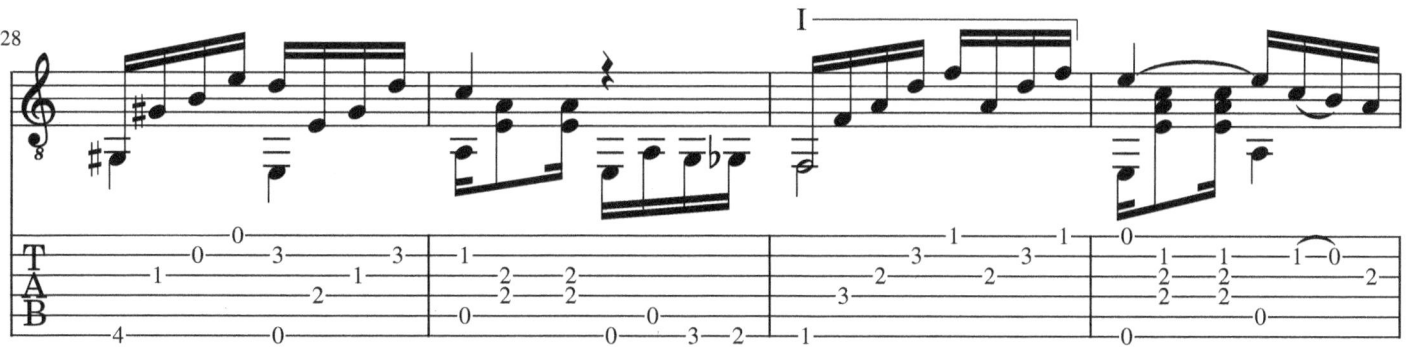

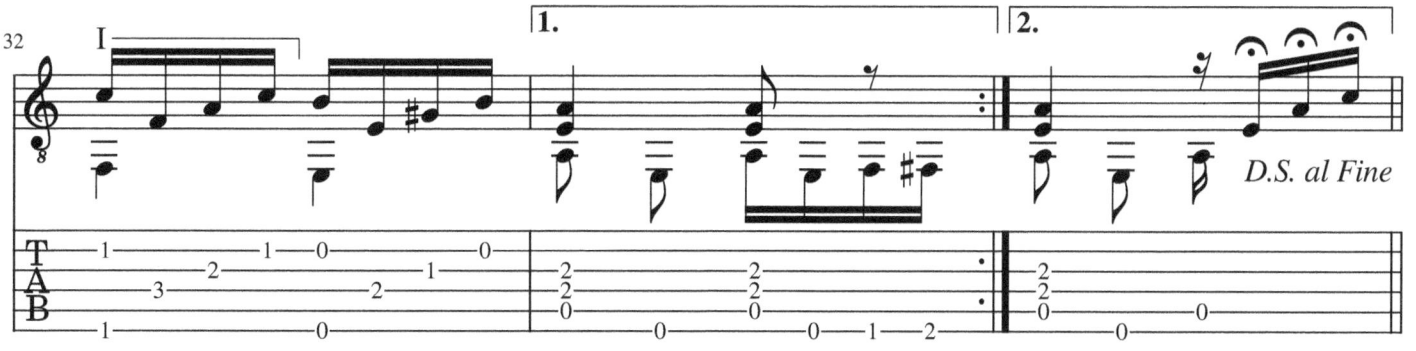

Cuban Dance

Anonymous

Romance
Spanish Romance

Anonymous

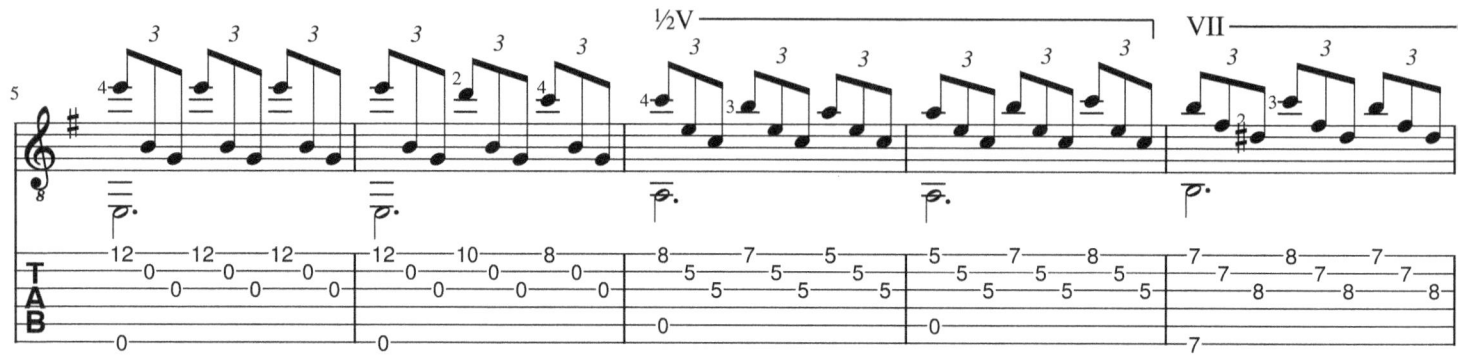
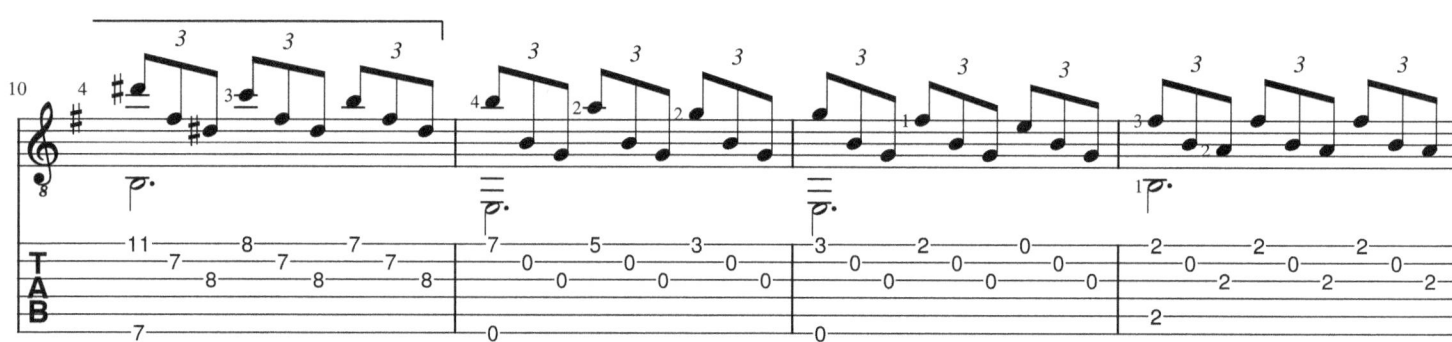
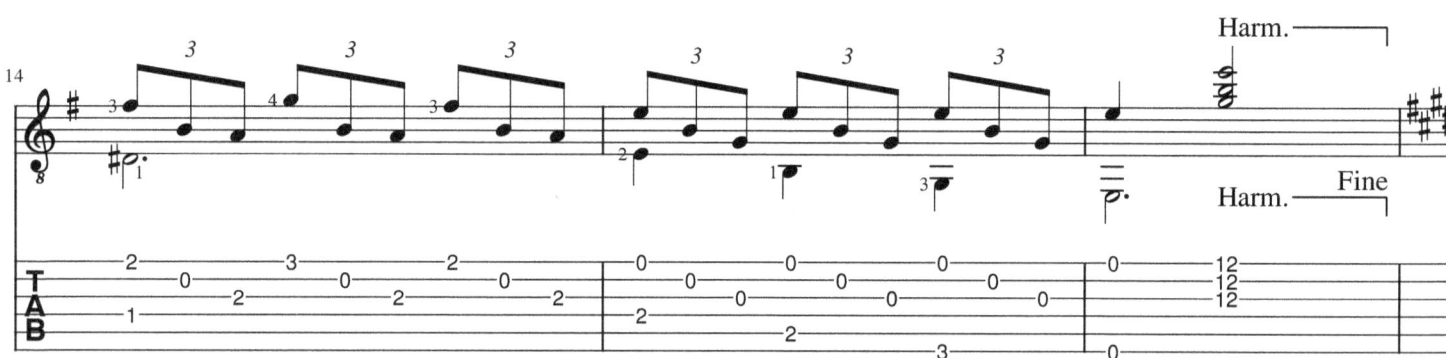

Choro

João Pernambuco (1883-1947)

Choro n°2

João Pernambuco (1883 - 1947)

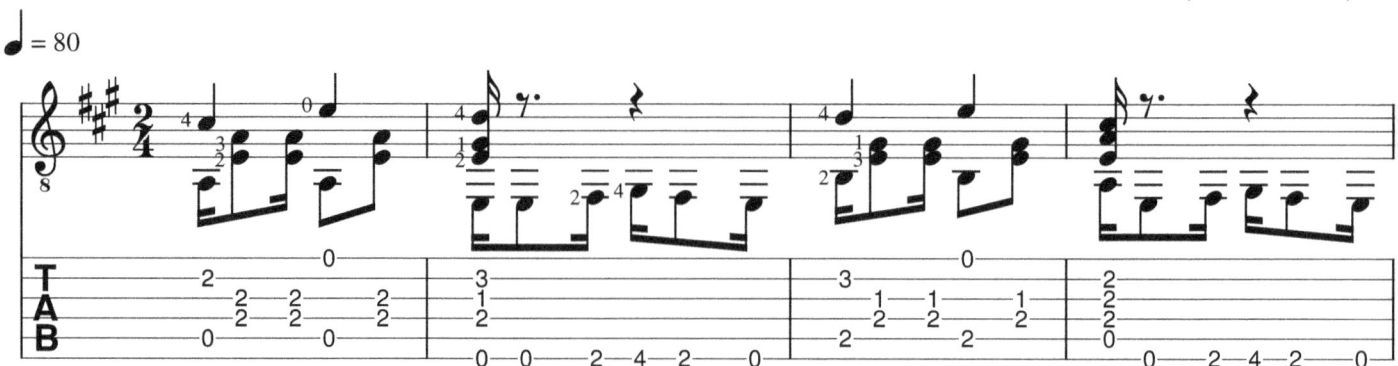
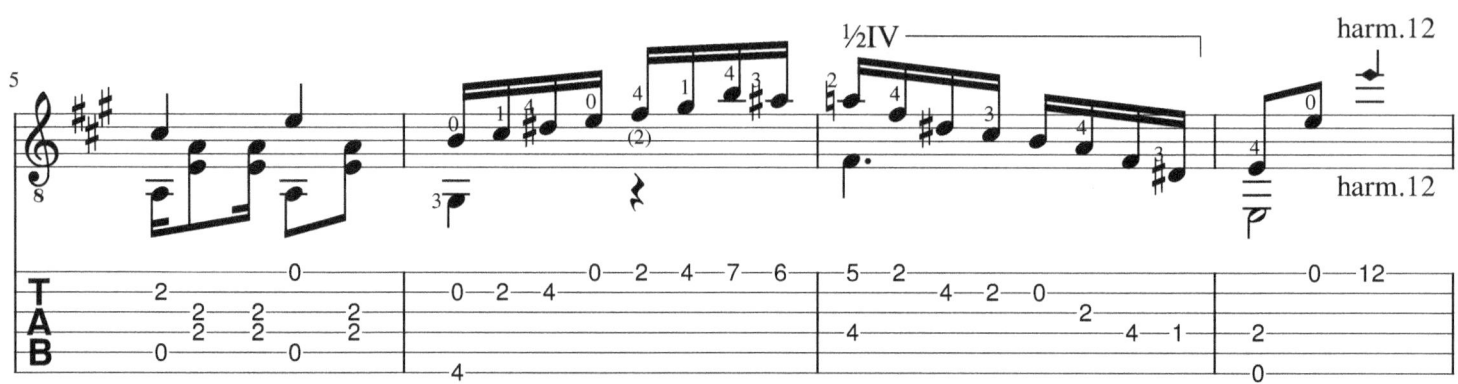
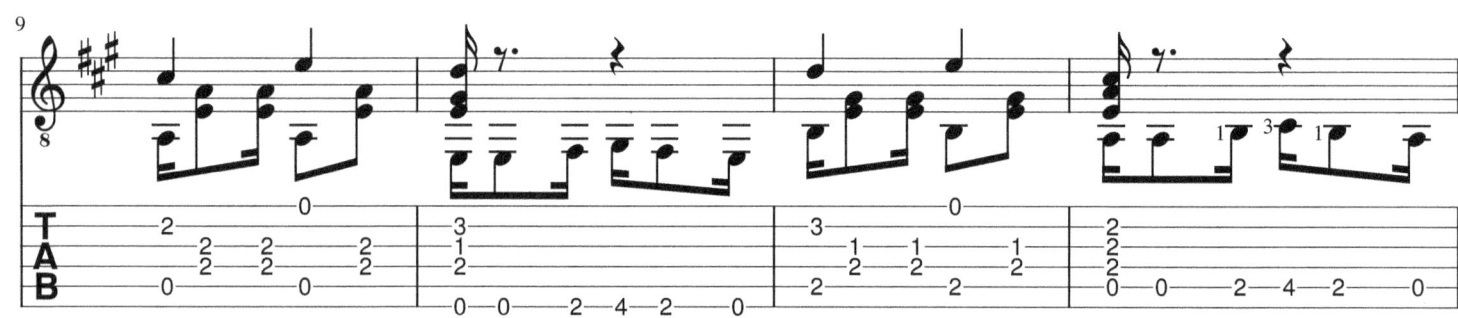
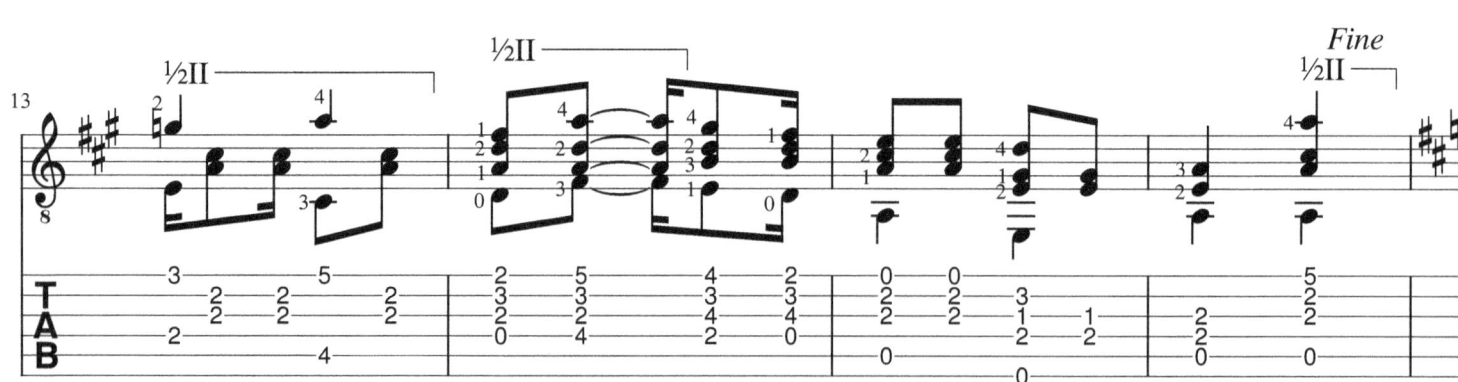

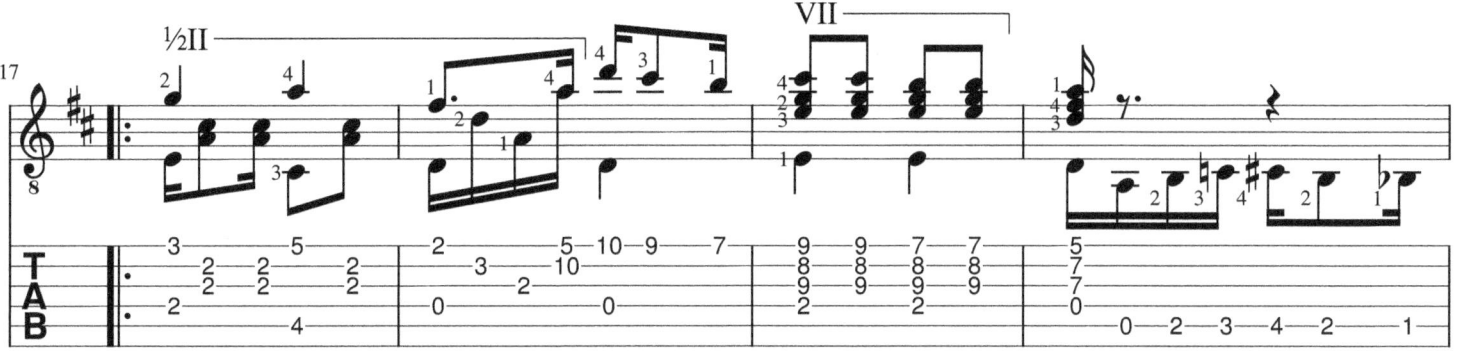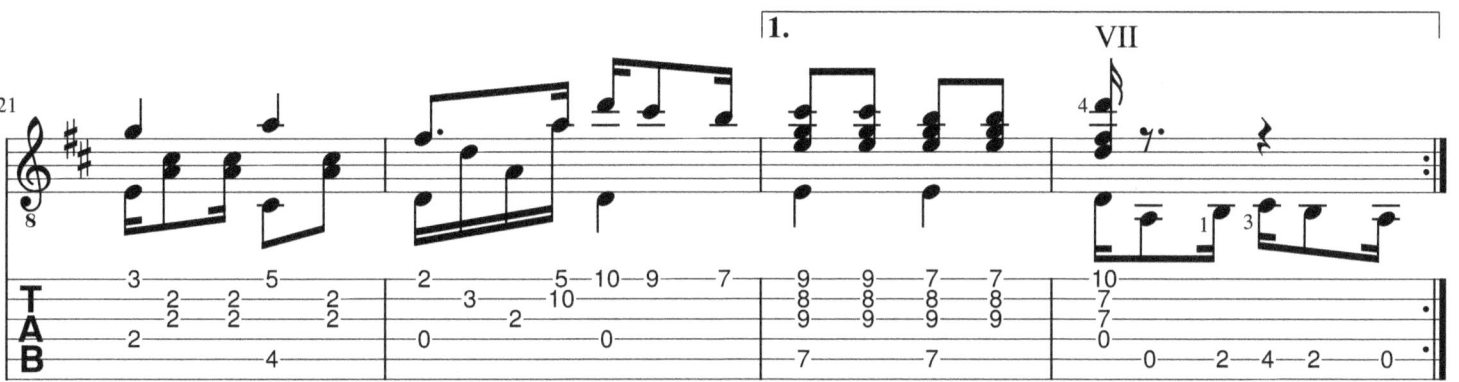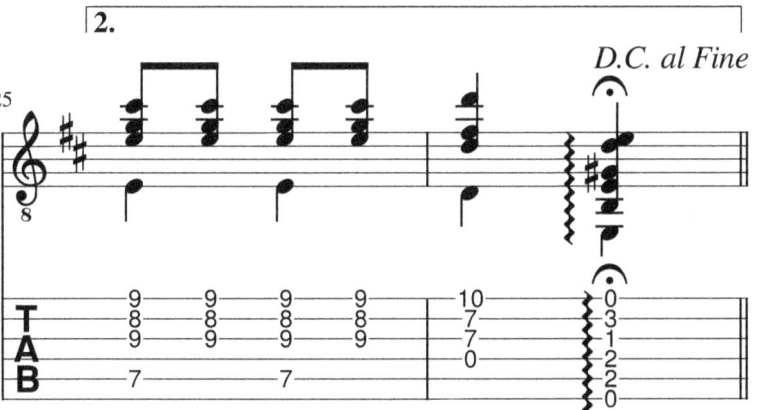

Lágrima
Tango

João Pernambuco (1883 - 1947)

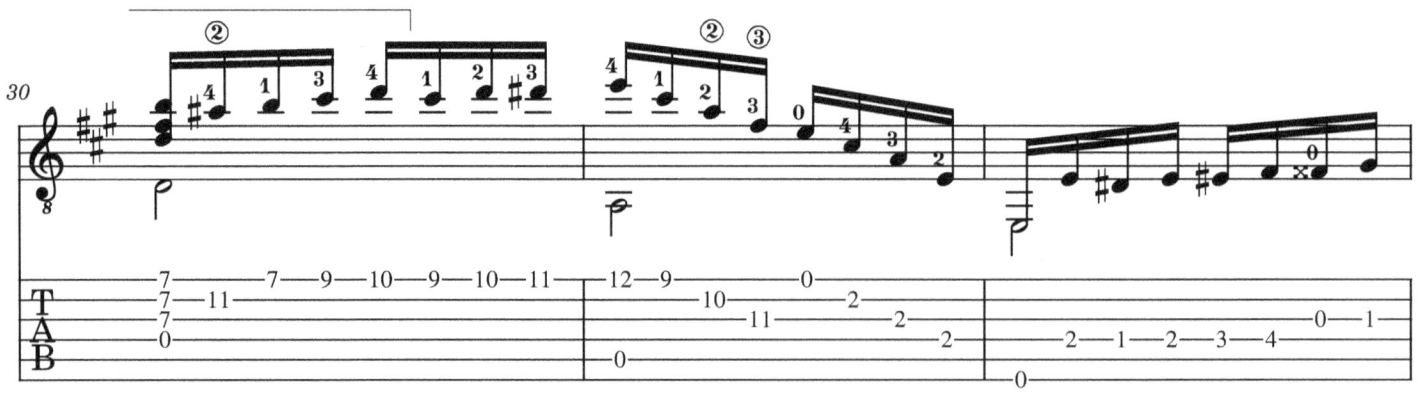
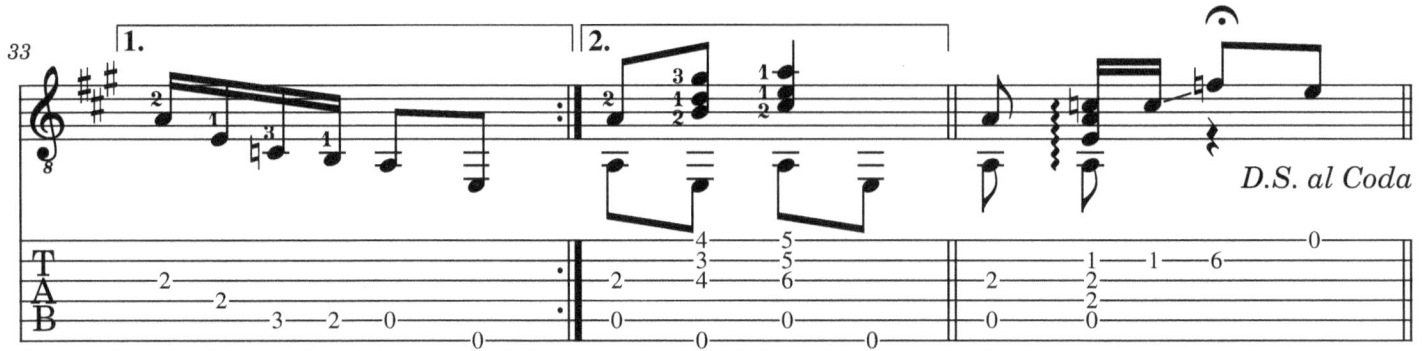
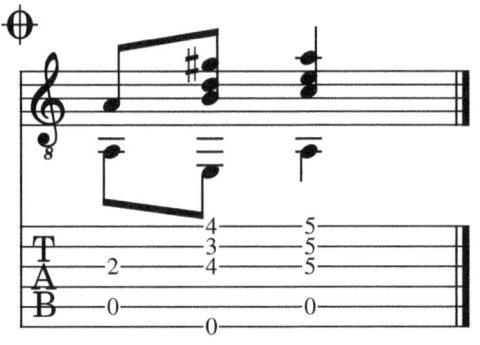

Yolanda

(Waltz)

Domingos Semenzato (1908-1993)

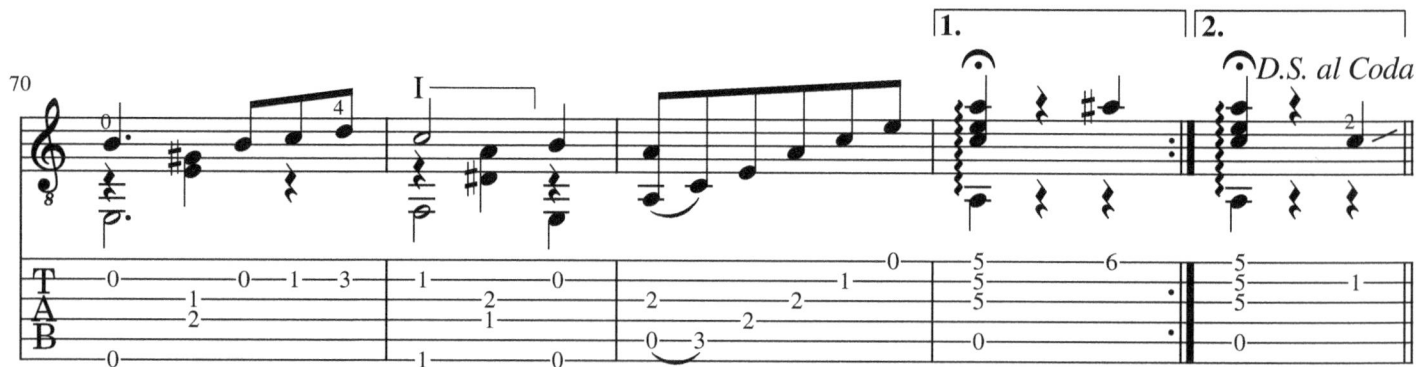
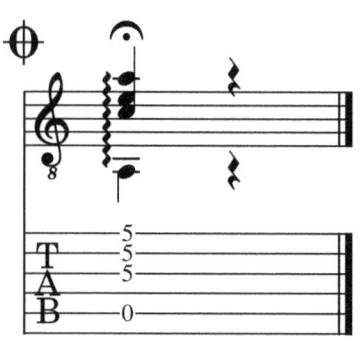

www.ingramcontent.com/pod-product-compliance
Lightning Source LLC
Chambersburg PA
CBHW041808070526
44585CB00026B/2880